LUDFORD BRIDGE
and
MORTIMER'S CROSS

THE WARS OF THE ROSES IN HEREFORDSHIRE
AND THE WELSH MARCHES,
AND THE ACCESSION OF
EDWARD IV

by

GEOFFREY HODGES

with drawings by
JOHN GIBBS

LOGASTON PRESS
1989

© Logaston Press 1989
© G. Hodges (Text) 1989
© John Gibbs (misericord illustrations) 1989

ISBN 0 9510242 2 1

All rights reserved. No part of this
publication may be reproduced, stored
in a retrieval system, or transmitted in
any form or by any means, electronic,
mechanical, photocopying, recording
or otherwise, without the prior permission,
in writing, of the publishers.

Logaston Press (publishers),
Woonton, Almeley, Herefordshire. HR3 6QH.

Set in 11 point on 13 Baskerville
Printed in Great Britain by Orphans Press, Leominster

For Gillian

Geoffrey Hodges is a historian who lives within easy reach of Ludford Bridge and Mortimer's Cross, and this coupled with an enquiring mind and delight in local history has led to a series of articles on these events. These have included pieces in the *Hereford Times* in 1982 and 1983, a paper for the *Woolhope Club Transactions* in 1982, pieces in the *Leominster Guide* for 1983 and 1988, *The Ricardian* (journal of the Richard III Society) in 1984 and the *Ludlow Historical Review* in 1987. In addition he advised Spot Video on the re-enactment of the Battle of Mortimer's Cross. Further research has led to this booklet which brings together and extends his views.

Acknowledgements

History can only be written by consulting the works of other people, so I am indebted to all writers and editors whose works are listed in the bibliography. My special thanks go to Lord Croft and his sister Mrs. Uhlman, for kindly allowing me to use Croft Castle Library; to Professor Ralph Griffiths (University College, Swansea) for kindly answering many queries and for many helpful suggestions; to Mr. and Mrs. Tonkin for help from their wide knowledge of the Woolhope Club Transactions; to Dr. Anthony Goodman and Dr. John Stephens (Edinburgh University) for some helpful advice; to the Librarians and staffs of the National Library of Wales (Aberystwyth), the Bodleian Library (Oxford), University College (London) and Hereford City Library; to the Director and staff of the Archives du Morbihan (Vannes, Brittany); to Mr. Richard Weaver and Miss Ann Radnor for some stimulating ideas on arms and armour; to Mr. Jimmy Moxon for some insights from the Great Civil War. I owe a great debt to my publishers, Mr. Andy Johnson and Mr. Steve Punter, both for valuable editorial advice and for indefatigably collecting so many excellent illustrations; to Mr. John Gibbs for his splendid heraldic drawings; to Miss Anne Sandford and staff at Hereford City Museum for kindly allowing the photograph of their fine set of contemporary weapons; to the Bodleian Library for the use of the illustration on the cover from Jean de Waurin's Manuscript (MS. Laud Misc. 653, fol. 11r.); to The Board of Trustees of the Royal Armouries at the Tower of London for photographs of armour and a bombard; finally to my family for their interest, tolerance and advice, particularly to Beth for her beautiful illustration of the Dragon of Cadwallader.

Introduction

Hart at rest, badge of Richard II

The civil war of 1459 to 1461 was the longest spell of fighting during the Wars of the Roses. Two of the seven battles took place in the neighbourhood of Ludlow and Wigmore, the heartland of Yorkist power: Ludford Bridge and Mortimer's Cross.

On 12 October 1459 two large armies met near Ludlow. The affair was known as the Rout of Ludford Bridge, because no battle was fought. Had battle been joined, the Yorkists would almost certainly have been overwhelmed by the greatly superior army of King Henry VI. With the battle lost and their leaders killed the course of history would have been very different. In the event, the Duke of York fled ignominiously with his sons the Earls of March and Rutland, and his allies the Earls of Salisbury and Warwick.

Historians know more about Ludford Bridge than about most of the other battles of the Wars of the Roses, though paradoxically few people have heard of it. Shakespeare omits Ludford from his plays on the Wars of the Roses; naturally, it has been forgotten by the people of Ludlow whose town was shamefully pillaged and ravished by the victors. It seems that even in the fifteenth century an unfought battle was less newsworthy than one resulting in terrible slaughter. However these can prove to be equally decisive, as is the case with Ludford, as it saw the effective end of the leadership of the Duke of York and the ascendancy of his son Edward and the Earl of Warwick.

The armies which met at Mortimer's Cross on 3 February 1461 were probably much smaller than those that had avoided each other two years earlier. Unlike Ludford Bridge everyone has heard of this 'obstinate, bloody and decisive battle,' as the monument at Kingsland calls it. As a result of his victory Edward, Earl of March and heir of the Mortimers, was proclaimed King of England, in London on 4 March. The monument goes too far, however, in saying that the battle fixed Edward on the throne. His position remained very precarious until his colossal victory over Queen Margaret's army at Towton on 29 March gave him unquestioned mastery.

Unlike Ludford, little is known about the battle of Mortimer's Cross. Throughout February attention in London was concentrated on the advance of the Queen's great northern army, fresh from Wakefield where the Duke of York was slaughtered. Panic rose to a pitch when she defeated the Earl of Warwick at St. Albans on 17 February; nonetheless she failed to take London and withdrew northwards. When Edward arrived in the capital a few weeks after his victory at Mortimer's Cross, the Londoners rapturously welcomed him as their deliverer. However, with the queen's army still a threat they were little interested in the battle which he had won in the remote and obscure Welsh Marches. The defeated Lancastrian commander at Mortimer's Cross was the Earl of Pembroke, Jasper

Tudor, uncle of the future Henry VII, and son of Owen Tudor, who was beheaded after the battle. Tudor propagandists not unnaturally played down such a disaster.

The battle of Mortimer's Cross has always seemed something of a sideshow, overshadowed by more spectacular events. One detail has, however, always attracted attention: the appearance in the sky before the battle of a parhelion, or three suns. Edward promptly called it an omen of Divine favour, and later adopted the Sun in Splendour as his device or badge. His accession to the throne is now firmly established by modern scholars as the moment when the fortunes of the English monarchy began to improve after the disastrous reign of Henry VI. Bosworth, where Henry Tudor won the crown in 1485, is much more famous than Mortimer's Cross, but the obscure battle from which 'this sun of York' made his way to the throne is just as significant an event.

This booklet pieces together what is surely one of the most extraordinary episodes in the history of England and Wales.

Causes of the Wars of the Roses

Antelope gorged and chained, personal badge of Henry VI

The English mediaeval monarchy was stable enough under a strong and capable king. On the other hand royal weakness, extravagance, incompetence or tyranny seem almost inevitably to have caused civil war. Henry VI succeeded his father, the strong and capable victor of Agincourt, as a babe in arms and was crowned King of France as well as of England, in which he is unique among English kings. As a boy, Henry impressed foreign ambassadors' with his intelligence, but he grew into a weak and obstinate man, easily influenced and ruinously extravagent. His colleges of Eton and King's Cambridge, contributed to his government's bankruptcy, even though he personally held not only the Crown lands, but also those of the Duchy of Lancaster, greatest of English feudal inheritances. During his long minority his uncle, John Duke of Bedford, was a very able regent until his death in 1435. Later, Henry's household and court were a greedy, violent and corrupt faction; justice was not carried out; he made an unpopular marriage to a dowerless French princess, Margaret of Anjou. To cap it all, France was lost, and with it control of the seas.

One of Henry's most hated advisers, the Duke of Suffolk, was blamed for the French marriage and the cession of Maine and Anjou, although in fact Henry himself was fully responsible for this policy of appeasing his French uncle, Charles VII. Similarly Edmund Beaufort, Duke of Somerset, was not entirely to blame for the loss of Normandy. During the 1440s Henry was an active blunderer, not the helpless creature of Shakespeare's plays, though he was always susceptible to bad advice.

Beaufort, as Henry's cousin, was the potential Lancastrian claimant to the throne if Henry and Margaret remained childless. The Beauforts were descended, like the Lancastrian kings, from John of Gaunt, the third of Edward III's five sons who reached manhood. Gaunt's mistress and third wife, Katherine Swynford, was the widow of one his retainers. Their four children born out of wedlock were legitimised by Richard II but debarred from the succession by Henry IV.

After the king himself the most important member of the royal family, and the greatest magnate, was Richard Plantagenet, Duke of York. His title came from his paternal grandfather, the fourth son of Edward III, and it brought him lands in the home counties, the east Midlands and the West Riding of Yorkshire. The greater part of Richard's revenues, though, came from the vast inheritance of his childless maternal uncle Edmund Mortimer, fifth Earl of March, who died of plague when serving as Lieutenant of Ireland in 1425. His estates were mostly in Wales, the Marches and Ireland. Edmund and Anne Mortimer, Richard's mother, were grandchildren of Philippa, daughter of Lionel, Duke of Clarence and Edward III's second son; Philippa's husband was Edmund Mortimer, third Earl of March. Richard Plantagenet was therefore 'heir general' to the throne; the Mortimer claim was arguably superior to those of either

Lancaster or York, but it had been ignored by Henry IV when he replaced Richard II as king. As the eldest legitimate grandson of Edward III, Henry was 'heir male'. Richard, Duke of York, did not assert his double claim, but the death in 1447 of Henry VI's uncle and heir, Humphrey Duke of Gloucester, made Richard heir presumptive. The lack of any absolute and definite rule governing the succession if a king had no son, helped fuel the struggle to come.

York's position was made even stronger because he had a growing family by his wife, Cecily Neville, whose mother was Joan Beaufort. Cecily's brother and nephew, the Earls of Salisbury and Warwick, later supported York. The Lancastrian prospects looked bleak. Henry was suspicious of York, a tactless and abrasive man who seems to have been generally unpopular. Despite his eminence as a magnate, Henry was determined to keep him from his rightful place on the royal council, which suited the incompetent favourite Somerset. Though Somerset had secured prompt repayment of money spent by him during his disastrous tour of duty in France, York was denied proper restitution for his much larger expenditure as lieutenant-general in Normandy. Finally, to get him out of the way, Henry sent York as lieutenant to Ireland.

In 1450 popular fury at bad government and lack of concern for general grievances erupted, and rocked the Lancastrian government to its foundations when Jack Cade and his Kentish rebels stormed London. The Duke of Suffolk and the Bishops of Chichester and Salisbury had previously been murdered; a similar fate now befell Lord Say, the Treasurer. The Duke of York returned from Ireland with the declared aim of reforming the government, not to seize the throne. He desperately needed, however, to obtain a resolution of the royal debts owed to him, so first had to thrust Somerset aside. To achieve this he felt compelled to resort to armed force; York's implacable hostility to Somerset was seen at the time to be a major immediate cause of civil war, nor has this verdict ever been in doubt.

York's military power lay mainly in Wales and the Marches. In the Middle Ages the Welsh Marches were an ill defined area on both sides of Offa's Dyke, where the Marcher Lords ruled almost as sovereign princes and the king's writ did not run. What was then called the principality, consisting of modern Gwynedd, Carmarthen and Cardigan, was under royal control. The Duke of York drew half his revenues and most of his military power from the old Mortimer lordships. His supporters were centred on a band of brothers, whose mother was Gwladys, daughter of Dafydd ap Llewelyn, better known as Davy Gam (the lame), who fell fighting for Henry V at Agincourt and who may have been the model for Shakespeare's delightful character Fluellen. Gwladys' first husband, Roger Vaughan of Bredwardine, had also fought at Agincourt; their sons were Watkin of Bredwardine, Thomas of Hergest and Roger of Tretower. She next married William ap Thomas, *y marchog las o Went* (the Blue Knight of Gwent), a senior officer and councillor to the Duke of York, and steward of his Welsh estates. Their sons were William, Richard and Thomas Herbert.

Sir William Herbert is one of the key characters of this story. Ruthless, unscrupulous, able and ambitious, he rose to great heights under Edward IV, whose second-in-command he was at Mortimer's Cross. He had served in France under the famous Welsh captain Matthew Gough, and had been knighted in 1453, together with Henry VI's half-brothers Edmund and Jasper Tudor. His chief colleagues were, besides his brothers, Sir Walter Devereux the elder of Weobley, who was constable of York's castle at Wigmore, together with his son, also called Walter, whose sister Anne he married.

The initial support of these and similar men gave York an army. Under the classical feudal system, land was held in exchange for military or labour service. Since the days of Edward I, however, English armies had consisted of men retained by legal indentures, or contracts, for wages, a logical extension of the cash economy which was gradually replacing feudal duties. A magnate would contract to serve the king in Scotland or France, with a following of knights and esquires whose own retainers served as men-at-arms or archers. Such armies had won the battles of Crécy and Agincourt. Mercenaries who had no feudal obligations were also employed, a practice as old as war itself; having few archers, the French had employed Genoese crossbowmen at Crécy. By 1450 there were probably comparatively few professional soldiers – 'men of war' – in the

English realm except in Wales and its Marches, the Scottish Marches, Ireland, and in Calais whose garrison was the only corps of truly professional soldiers available to the King of England.

In England, nobles and gentry took indentured retainers into their service, both as soldiers and as household servants, councillors, legal advisers and administrators of their lands. The gentry were vital both to the magnates and to the king; they served the magnates as soldiers and officials, and the king as sheriffs, justices of the peace, coroners and managers of his household and lands. The shire appointments were liable to fall under the control of magnates, especially under the weak rule of Henry VI, so that government came to be exercised through these families, or affinities, of landowners. The king had an immense amount of patronage at his disposal, but weak kings like Henry gave it out heedlessly, so that key appointments easily got into the wrong hands: a sheriff who was the creature of an unscrupulous magnate could brow beat juries, or empanel biased ones; Parliament could be packed in the interest of a factious court like that of Henry VI.

The system which grew out of the indentured retinues of the Hundred Years War has the derogatory name of 'bastard feudalism' and historians are divided about how baneful its influence was. Retainers sported the livery badges of their lords, familiar to us as inn-signs like the Red Lion, White Hart, White Swan, Feathers, Talbot, Bear or Blue Boar. This produced a trend towards violence, something like the feuding of so-called supporters of modern football clubs. Even as late as 1642 men were also raised for military service by commissions of array, a sort of conscription of the lower social orders as in Shakespeare's hilarious description of Falstaff's recruiting in Henry IV, Part II, but they often proved unwilling and unreliable.

Thus if a noble or gentleman was given to lawlessness, like the Duke of Norfolk, the Earl of Devon or Sir William Herbert, private war broke out. Many ugly examples are known, but the most serious, which led to the bloody clash at St. Albans, was that between the two great northern affinities: Northumberland and the Nevilles. With a king as feeble as Henry VI, whose own household was a byword for law-breaking, the causes of the Wars of the Roses become clearer. Though the Duke of York is regarded as comparatively law-abiding by some but not all historians, he resorted to force when he could not secure the redress of his grievances by constitutional means.

The Rout of Ludford Bridge

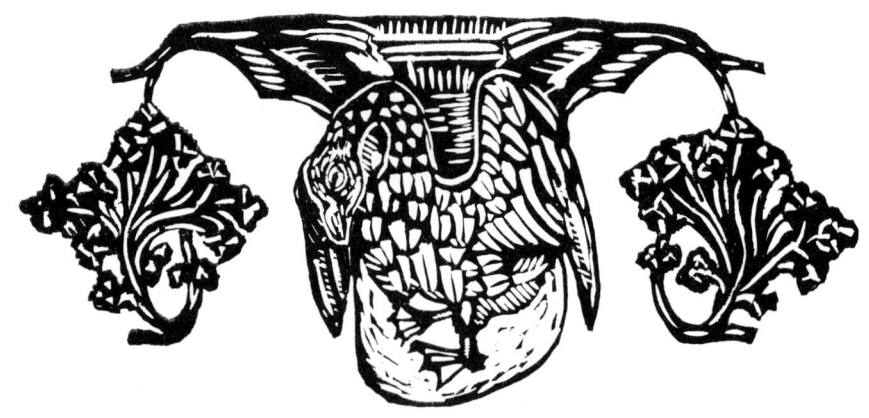

de Bohun White Swan, badge of Henry VI

York's first armed protest and attempt to oust Somerset as chief adviser to the king ended ignominiously at Dartford in 1452, an event which, though bloodless, perhaps marks the start of the Wars of the Roses. It also foreshadows Ludford Bridge in several ways. York showed himself as an inept politician, as he was supported only by the Earl of Devon and Lord Cobham, for it was madness to rebel against an anointed king without massive support from the peerage. This support simply did not exist, nor was York the man to cultivate it; he was distrusted by the other magnates, however much they might deplore his treatment or dislike the court party. At Dartford York constructed a fortified camp, defended with guns, in the modern manner of warfare, but faced by a greatly superior royal army, he was forced to submit. The common explanation for York's actions is that he was tricked into surrender by being falsely informed that Somerset was a prisoner. In fact the king had proclaimed his confidence in his favourite, and had denounced York as a rebel. In truth Somerset's position was impregnable, and York was denied access to the king to present his grievances, which only increased his distrust of both king and court, making civil war all the more likely.

In 1453 events began to move York's way. John Talbot, Earl of Shrewsbury, who was the greatest English soldier of the day and who had been with the king at Dartford, was now sent on a hopeless mission to recover Gascony, and perished with most of his army at Castillon, to the east of Bordeaux. This disaster was immediately followed by Henry's first total mental collapse which lasted for eighteen months. The discrediting of Somerset over events in France and the inability of the king to manage affairs allowed York to take his rightful place as Protector, taking the opportunity to send Somerset to the Tower. But then at last the queen produced a son; Henry recovered his reason and Somerset his liberty. York meanwhile had formed an alliance with the powerful northern Neville earls, his brother-in-law Salisbury and his nephew Warwick, the future kingmaker, whom he had helped in their private war with their rival the Earl of Northumberland, head of the Percy clan. In addition Warwick had his own quarrel with Somerset over the lordship of Glamorgan. The absence of effective royal discipline and justice inevitably meant that nobles and gentry resorted to violence whenever there were disputes over land ownership.

In 1455 these Yorkist lords were summoned to face a Great Council of king and peers at Leicester, where they would probably have been arrested and charged with treason. Rather than risk this, they marched on London. They defeated and killed Somerset and Northumberland at the first battle of St. Albans, really just a murderous brawl in the streets, as only about sixty men were killed. Still, politically it was decisive, because with blood to avenge the heirs of the slaughtered lords joined the queen, and the quarrel became more implacable than ever. Though York became Protector again, his military success had if anything weakened his political position, and the queen was soon able to dismiss his government.

Following the practice of the French kings, who could rule France without Paris, Queen Margaret now moved the court from the hostile capital to Coventry, whose loyalty and central position in the Lancastrian midlands offered short-term advantages. With Coventry and most of the midlands in royalist hands, Warwick's influence now counted for little outside Warwick Castle. The northwest with Lancaster at its heart was royalist, as was Cheshire, for the queen's young son was Earl of Chester and the Cheshire gentry maintained a strong hold over North Wales. However, in the long term failure to control London proved fatal to the Lancastrian dynasty. Not only was the city the seat of majesty and of government, but it was the commercial capital, and so a source of finance, whilst its population furnished soldiers. Meanwhile Dublin was loyal to York, and Warwick was Captain of Calais.

By 1456 William Herbert had gained a violent reputation in the southern Marches, and in August of that year the Herberts, Vaughans, Devereux (father and son), and many other gentry of Herefordshire and adjacent parts, invaded South Wales with an army of about 2,000 men. Their aim was to assert York's authority, though York was then leading an expedition against Scotland. They occupied the royal castles of Carmarthen, Carreg Cennan, Cardigan and Aberystwyth, held by Gruffydd ap Nicholas, another lawless character who was formerly a retainer of the late Duke of Somerset. Before his death, Somerset had been constable of these castles; York had taken over as constable during his second term as Protector, but the military success of his retainers led to another political disaster. Edmund Tudor, who had also been trying to bring Gruffydd to order from his base at Pembroke, died and was replaced by his brother Jasper, a much more forceful man. York was made to lease the castles to him. The queen skilfully divided York's Welsh from his English followers by pardoning the former, notably the Herberts and Vaughans, and punishing the others, notably the two Devereux, John Lingen of Sutton, James Baskerville of Eardisley, and Thomas Monington of Sarnesfield with fines, imprisonment and recognizances – orders binding them to keep the peace.

Jasper Tudor built up a royalist power block based on his control of the main castles of south-west Wales, and Gruffydd ap Nicholas and his sons became Jasper's retainers. So too did Sir John Scudamore of Kentchurch in Herefordshire, his sons and his brother Sir William. John and William Scudamore were grandsons of Owain Glyn Dwr, one of whose principal enemies in South Wales had been Davy Gam, whose family supported York. Any quarrel between two gentry families in those days inevitably led each to seek the protection – 'good lordship' – of a magnate, and the blood-letting which followed Mortimer's Cross was, perhaps, mainly caused by this feud between two Welsh family groupings or affinities.

William Herbert and others of his affinity were not only pardoned for their parts in the 1456 affair, but also given offices under the crown. This not only bound them to the queen, but might also have made it easier for her and Jasper to prevent further feuding between the Herbert-Vaughan axis, and that of Gruffydd and Scudamore. The court's handling of this situation cleverly undermined York's position in this vital area.

In 1459 the queen and her advisers decided that the time was ripe finally to crush the Yorkists. The Duke of York and the Nevilles were pointedly excluded from a great council at Coventry in June. From this they rightly concluded that the council would condemn them for treason, and once again resorted to a muster of their forces, so as to present their grievances to the king. York was at Ludlow with his two elder sons, Edward Earl of March and Edmund Earl of Rutland, together with his wife and their two younger sons.

The royalist decision to engineer this crisis was a shrewd one and was probably based on two considerations. First, York's retainers in the southern Marches were very unlikely to help him: the Herberts and Vaughans now enjoyed royal favour, whereas Devereux and the other Herefordshire gentry were too cowed. Secondly, the queen and her allies had been less than successful in their attempts to winkle Warwick out of Calais; his position there as captain, and his spectacular acts of piracy which were necessary to pay his men, were a growing diplomatic embarrassment to the government. They also made Warwick something of a national hero, especially among the warlike men of Kent, and to all who were disgusted at the humiliating experiences of the last twenty years. Not only had the French driven the English out, but they currently seemed able to raid the coasts and seaports of England with impunity.

Now, however, Warwick was compelled to come to York's aid. He brought with him troops of the Calais garrison under their master porter Andrew Trollope: 'a very subtle man of war' in the view of the Burgundian chronicler Jean de Waurin. Trollope was an esquire (from the French *escuyer,* meaning shield bearer) with long experience of warfare in France, and a pirate whose exploits produced much protest in official records. Despite Warwick's reputation few of his midland tenants seem to have joined him, and he narrowly escaped an ambush en route to Ludlow near Coventry, laid by the young Duke of Somerset.

Meanwhile Warwick's father, the Earl of Salisbury, who was Warden of the West March towards Scotland, could call on hardened fighting men from that theatre of war and with a small but tough retinue he marched from Middleham Castle in the West Riding. As he crossed Staffordshire, the queen made a determined attempt to stop him. Waiting with her main army, including King Henry, at Eccleshall, she sent a force of Cheshire men led by Lord Audley against Salisbury, after the young Prince of Wales had issued the force with the Lancastrian livery badge of the White Swan, formerly a device of the Bohun earls of Hereford, the king's ancestors. Audley threw his army in Salisbury's way at Blore Heath, between Newcastle-under-Lyme and Market Drayton, on 23 September 1459. Salisbury fought his way clear in a bloody encounter in which Audley and many gentlemen of Cheshire were killed, but his own losses were considerable, two of his sons being taken prisoner. He then narrowly avoided the main royal army and joined York and Warwick at Ludlow.

The Yorkist leaders now moved forward to Worcester, where they took the sacrament in the cathedral, sending the prior to the king with the usual list of grievances, which was as always ignored. Henry was probably not shown the list, for by now his mind is thought to have been beyond coping with political problems. However, there are signs that he was angered by the affront to his livery of the Swan at Blore Heath and encouraged the army to action; the Swan was an emblem which he had presented in the past not only to his servants, but also to eminent foreigners like knights from the Italian city of Mantua.

The Yorkists declined battle on the road to Kidderminster, and fell back on Tewkesbury, perhaps hoping that a long and tortuous march might shake off the vastly superior royal army, or even cause it to break up: 'the king was more than 30,000 of harnessed men, beside naked men that were compelled for to come with the king.' Here the anonymous continuator of Gregory's Chronicle, always ready with interesting details, exaggerates like most of his kind, but it is clear that the royal army was large and made up of the retinues of, maybe, twenty peers. The king is thought to have had with him the Dukes of Buckingham, Somerset and Exeter, the Earls of Northumberland, Shrewsbury, Devon, Wiltshire and Arundel, Viscount Beaumont, and five barons for certain, including the new Lord Audley. Despite having been with York at Dartford, the Earl of Devon had now joined the court party after the two men had quarrelled over the handling of inter-family disputes in Devon. Jasper Tudor, Earl of Pembroke, was probably policing Wales but arrived in Coventry with his retinue shortly after the taking of Ludlow, in time for the parliament which condemned the rebels.

'Harnessed men' meant the fee'd and liveried retainers of these lords, wearing varying amounts of body armour; the 'naked men' were probably mostly followers rather than fighting men, pressed into service by commissions of array. Gregory is thought to have gained experience of war with Warwick's foot soldiers at the second battle of St. Albans, then still in the future on 17 February 1461; amongst other military observations he says that 'the substance that got that field were household men and fee'd men.' In other words, what counted were the retinues, products of bastard feudalism, which made up an army. However it seems clear that, at Ludford Bridge, the king had up to twice the number of household men that were available to the Yorkists, who were in Gregory's phrase 'over weak.' We may perhaps think of a royal army numbering 12,000 or more, with the Yorkists only half as strong.

The Earl of Salisbury had been excluded from the pardon offered at Worcester, perhaps because he had killed some of the king's men at Blore Heath. York and Warwick were hardly likely to rely much on the queen's promises of pardon, so they withdrew through Ledbury and Leominster, with the royal army tramping ominously after them, about a day's march behind. Henry was later praised in the Coventry Act of Attainder for 'not sparing for any impediment or difficulty of way, nor of intemperance of weathers.' During a campaign of thirty days duration he 'lodged in bare field sometime two nights together with all your Host in the cold season of the year.' Whatever his mental weaknesses, the evidence is that physically Henry was a strong man, with notable powers of endurance, as shown during his years of wandering in the north before his capture in 1465. He was also keen on hunting. It is thus not incredible that he may have been able to wear armour, mount a horse and go through the motions of being a warrior king. There is even reason to think that on this occasion he showed some stirrings of resolution.

The impression of a wet and cold autumn is enhanced by details of the final road to Ludlow: what with 'the impediment of the ways and straitness, and by let of waters, it was nigh even' on 12 October before the royal positions were taken up on the Ludford meadows, banners displayed and tents pitched. The 'let of waters' suggests flooding by the River Lugg at the north end of Leominster, assisted by the Pinsley brook. The route taken seems to have been the line of the modern B4361 through Luston and Richards Castle, for the present A road into Ludlow from the south dates from after 1756, as is indicated by the turnpike cottage at the modern junction with the B road. The old route went from Overton past Huck's Barn, to the left of the present road, which it then crossed, going to the right of Ludford House and then joining the line of Ludford village street. The present cutting going down to the bridge was part of the realignment made by the turnpike trust in the eighteenth century.

Under mediaeval conditions and in very wet weather, this switchback route, crossing the grain of the country, could well have been very slow going. We are also told that the Yorkists 'being in the same fields the same day and place, traitorously ranged in battle, fortified their chosen ground, their carts with guns set before their battles (battalions), made their skirmishes, laid their embushments there, suddenly to have taken the advantage of your Host.' This suggests the use of harassing tactics back along the road to Leominster, as the Yorkist redoubt across the Ludford meadows must have been conspicuous to the royalist mounted scouts or scurriers. Gregory says: 'the Duke of York let make a great deep ditch and fortified it with guns, carts and stakes.' The exact position of this battery will probably never be known, as aerial photographs show that the area was covered by the barrack blocks of a military hospital during the Second World War, but if the battery had followed the line of the modern farm road to the south of Ludford House, there would have been a good field of fire for the guns.

We may imagine the royal camp, with the banners of the king and his lords flapping damply on a wet autumn afternoon, visible to most of York's army, whose morale was evidently low. To the mediaeval mind, the idea of fighting against the king in person was sacrilegious. The belated discovery of the king's presence at St. Albans had caused dismay, especially when it was also known that he had been slightly wounded by an arrow. The reign of Henry VI had been disastrous and his character was ineffectual, but he had that aura of majesty which was still revered in Shakespeare's day. At Ludford it really seems that his presence, coupled with the overwhelming superiority of his army, took the heart out of the rebels.

The planting of a banner was a challenge to the enemy and an appeal to God for victory. It could be followed by negotiations between heralds, as frequently happened, though there is no mention of any last minute peace-making attempts here. Guns were discharged at random into the gathering dusk, but it was the tactics of Dartford again with the same military and political weaknesses. Just twelve months after Dartford there had been a devastating demonstration of the power of guns dug in behind an earthwork, when Talbot's army was shattered at Castillon. Ironically, his son was now present at Ludford to see York holding an extended front with too few men; at Castillon the French had had their new professional army, plenty of men, and the best artillery and gunners in Europe.

Very likely the Yorkist soldiers had been encouraged to expect a goodly number of Marchmen and Welshmen under Herbert,

Vaughan and Devereux. In the event, only the younger Devereux had arrived. Maybe that evening men were already beginning to slink away in the gathering gloom, despite the spreading of rumours that the king was dead and that masses were being said for his soul. The final blow now fell. Part of the vanguard of York's army consisted of Warwick's Calais troops, and Andrew Trollope now led most of these over to the royalists on receipt of a letter from the Duke of Somerset, of whom he had formerly been a companion in arms. Gregory says that this defection took place near Coventry, Trollope seeing that 'the Earl of Warwick was going unto the Duke of York, and not unto the king'; it is now more generally agreed that it was at Ludford. The chroniclers Fabyan and Hall say that since Trollope knew all the plans of the Yorkists, the latter felt that the matter was now hopeless. A council was held then and there. The troops would probably refuse to fight. If they did the result would be annihilation. The councillors may well have urged York and the earls to fly as the only means of saving their party, but whether the advice was offered or not, fly they did. 'Almighty God,' in the scatheing words of the Act of Attainder, '... smote the hearts of the said Duke and Earls suddenly from the most presumptuous pride, to the most shameful fall of cowardice that could be thought, so that about midnight ... they stole away out of the field, under colour they would have refreshed them awhile in the town of Ludlow, leaving their Standards and Banners in their battle directly against your field, fled out of the town unarmed, with few persons into Wales.'

A heavily packed parliament assembled early in November at Coventry which passed the Act of Attainder against York and his party, stripping them of all their lands and offices, declaring them traitors, and debarring their heirs from succeeding them. Nothing so devastating had been done to so many of the landed class before, even by Richard II who had finished by confiscating the duchy of Lancaster from the future Henry IV. It had always been assumed that the heir of a convicted traitor should not suffer for his father's sins. The Act included York, his two sons, the Neville earls, the Countess of Salisbury, Salisbury's two sons, two minor barons, and seventeen knights and esquires. Of these only Walter Devereux, esquire, of Weobley, represented York's southern Marcher affinity. Richard Croft of Croft Castle and members of the Harper family of Wellington near Hereford, were pardoned for some disorderly behaviour soon afterwards, but there is no evidence that they were at Ludford. We are told how many of the convicted men, including Devereux, came to the king to beg for their lives, in shirts and carrying halters like the burghers of Calais before Edward III. They were granted their lives, but not their estates. The Duchess of York 'came unto King Henry and submitted her unto his grace' and she was placed in the custody of her sister, the Duchess of Buckingham.

York's political judgement may by now have been very seriously questioned; the outcome of Ludford could have destroyed all faith in his leadership. Two immediate consequences stand out sharply. First, the principal sufferers were York's own people of Ludlow and its district, who had presumably trusted in his protection. Instead, he had drawn down the wrath of the court party upon them and they now suffered the ultimate degradation of their town being sacked by the victors. 'The misrule of the king's gallants at Ludlow,' wrote Gregory, 'when they had drunken enough of wine that was in taverns and other places, they full ungodly smote out the heads of the pipes and hogsheads of wine, that men went wetshod in wine, and then they robbed the town, and bare away bedding, cloth, and other stuff, and defiled many women.'

Secondly, although the Yorkist chiefs fled that very night, they made for separate destinations. York, Rutland and Lord Clinton escaped safely to Dublin where York was lieutenant, though they were closely pursued through Wales, perhaps by Jasper's men. Warwick returned to Calais which had been held for him by his uncle Lord Fauconberg, and he was accompanied by his father and also his cousin, Edward Earl of March.

Edward undoubtedly understood the strategic and commercial importance of Calais, where England, France and Burgundy met, and whence the Channel could be controlled. Warwick may well have convinced him already that, if the Ludford campaign miscarried, Calais was by far the most promising base for any Yorkist counter-offensive. Also, by parting with his father at this juncture, Edward may have been expressing a loss of confidence which could have been general.

The big fish had escaped the net spread for them by the queen, but her followers could now help themselves freely to the forfeited lands: the resulting issues of patents in the Chancery records give us a good idea of which peers contributed to the rout of Ludford Bridge. It may be fairly called the last triumph of the House of Lancaster, as never again did Henry VI ride with his host to any kind of military success.

Ludford Bridge was an appalling disaster for Richard, Duke of York, a fiasco from which it is hard to see that he could ever recover. The impression is that it ruined his prestige and credibility, which had suffered enough from the successive humiliations which had befallen him from Dartford onwards. Nowhere can this eclipse have been more serious than in the Welsh Marches, his political heartland, which he had so signally failed to defend. His own heir apparently saw no future in following him to Dublin. York spent the next ten months there, presumably brooding over his wrongs, with only Clinton and Rutland, his ineffectual second son, to soothe his mental anguish. None of his trusted councillors were with him, nor his wife, towards whom Henry showed some generosity, allowing her to keep some of her husband's manors, including several in Herefordshire; for example Pembridge, Kingsland and Orleton. York's situation cannot have helped him to look at matters more realistically than he had done in the past, and effective leadership of the Yorkists now passed to Warwick at Calais.

Yorkist Recovery and Crisis

Falcon and Fetterlock, personal badge of Richard, Duke of York

As a political manager Richard Neville, Earl of Warwick, was a genius, perhaps one of the greatest in our history. He knew how to find out what men were thinking and how to win their support. He understood the principle immortalised by Dickens in the Eatanswill election: a man was welcome to take out of Warwick's kitchen as much meat as he could stick on his dagger. He was adept at disseminating propaganda and at stirring up sedition. On the military front his buccaneering exploits proved him a fearless fighting man, a champion of national interests and keeper of the seas. Yet as a commander in the field he proved timid and indecisive. He was finally to overreach himself because of his ruthless and megalomaniac ambition; his attempt to restore Henry VI and depose Edward ended in disaster. Edward was finally able to outwit, outfight and utterly destroy Warwick at the battle of Barnet in 1471.

In March 1460 Warwick visited York in Dublin, no doubt in order to plan strategy, and York seems to have given full approval to Warwick's plans. In June the Yorkist lords seized Sandwich, and after a triumphal march through Kent they entered London peacefully on 2 July. Warwick's hand can surely be seen in a manifesto of the Duke of York's grievances, and in a ballad pinned to the gates of Canterbury, for whilst a verse of this gives a line of praise each to Salisbury, Edward and Fauconberg, two lines are given to 'that noble knight and flower of manhood, Richard earl of Warwick, shield of our defence.'

The Tower of London was well provisioned and held by Lord Scales, Lord Hungerford and other royalists. Salisbury remained to direct the siege, while Warwick, Edward and Fauconberg set out to meet the king at Northampton. They were accompanied by the Prior of St. John, the Archbishop of Canterbury (whose brother had married York's sister), and several other barons and bishops, including the papal legate, Francesco Coppino, Bishop of Terni. There was now at last a chance of negotiating with the king from a position of spiritual as well as of temporal power, such as York had never been able to arrange.

Pope Pius II, who wanted a crusade to recover Constantinople from the Turks, had sent Coppino to England to win support. The Italian states were also concerned that the French monarchy would use its growing power to intervene in Italy, where two branches of the Valois dynasty had claims: Anjou to the Kingdom of Naples and Sicily, and Orleans to Milan, which was then held by the most successful mercenary captain of the age, Francesco Sforza; he had also married the heiress of the last duke, whose title he now took. Coppino was in correspondence with Sforza, the more confidential passages being in invisible ink, recommending support for the Yorkist lords, of whom Warwick was the acknowledged leader. He suggested that if the Yorkists directed King Henry VI's affairs, rather than Margaret of Anjou and her grasping courtiers, England might try to recover Normandy and Gascony, which would discourage

French aggression in Italy. The Milanese diplomatic papers clearly show Warwick's predominance in the unfolding English drama, of which they convey a vivid sense and give us our earliest account, even though they are inaccurate owing to the great difficulty of getting information.

Henry VI seems to have reverted to his usual passive resignation after his almost militant mood at Ludford. On 10 July 1460 the Yorkists found him near Northampton in a strong entrenchment defended by cannon, and whose ditches may have been flooded from the River Nene. It was very like Ludford but with the positons reversed, and the military disadvantages of a rigid defensive position with its back to a river was probably not lost on Edward. The Duke of Buckingham was in command, as he had been at St. Albans; he refused the peaceful overtures of the Yorkist barons and bishops, denying them access to the king's person and declaring that 'the Earl of Warwick shall not come to the king's presence, and if he come he shall die.' Heavy rain put the royal guns out of action and the Yorkists easily stormed the works, aided by a traitor, Lord Grey of Ruthin – another parallel with Ludford. The king was taken unharmed, but Buckingham was killed along with two lords, recently named by York as 'our mortal and extreme enemies' – the new Earl of Shrewsbury and Viscount Beaumont. Lord Egremont, a son of the late Earl of Northumberland, whose violence had been the immediate cause of his father's strife with the Nevilles, was also killed.

A third 'mortal and extreme enemy' who was not present at Northampton was the prominent courtier James Butler, Earl of Wiltshire and also head of an Irish clan and Earl of Ormond. He had escaped at St. Albans disguised as a monk, one of those who 'left their harness behind them cowardly,' as it is said in the famous letters of the Paston family. The writer of Gregory's Chronicle is even more scatheing, saying that Wiltshire 'fought mainly with the heels, for he was afraid of losing of beauty.' He had been Lieutenant of Ireland but was now Treasurer, had been present at Ludford, and in June 1460, just before the Yorkist invasion, had together with Scales and Hungerford participated in an ugly act of terrorism in which the Duke of York's town of Newbury had suffered the fate of

Ludlow, without the same provocation. Wiltshire made himself scarce as soon as the Yorkists landed, fleeing to Holland, and whilst his subsequent movements concern this story deeply, they are veiled in obscurity. Scales was killed by the infuriated Londoners when fleeing from the Tower after its surrender to Salisbury, for having fired its guns indiscriminately into the city. The outrageous events at Ludlow, Newbury and the Tower easily explain popular hatred for the Lancastrians in the Welsh Marches and the South East.

As after St. Albans, so after Northampton, a Yorkist government was set up under an obedient king. Only nine months after Ludford Bridge Lancastrian rule was over, incredible though that might seem. Warwick at once sent orders to the leading Yorkists in the southern Welsh Marches who were prompt to resume their old allegiance: Sir William Herbert, his half-brother Roger Vaughan, Walter Devereux (whose father Sir Walter had died in 1459), James Baskerville, Richard Croft, Thomas Monington, and Henry ap Gruffydd of Vowchurch in the Golden Valley.

These orders were to arrest Lancastrians in Herefordshire, specifically two members of the last parliament, Sir John Barre and Thomas Fitzharry. What happened to Barre is not clear, but Fitzharry, a lawyer, made his way to Jasper Tudor. The fact that Warwick's principal commission was also addressed to Edward Earl of March, and to several Shropshire gentry, does not alter the impression that the Yorkist centre of gravity lay in Herefordshire, which provided most of Edward's companions at Mortimer's Cross. The evidence for this comes from a book by William Worcester, a contributor to the Paston letters, which mentions Herbert, Devereux, Vaughan and Croft, as well as Henry ap Gruffyd, described as 'a man of war', who had been pardoned and rewarded by the court after his part in the rebellion of 1456. Though Worcester does not mention Baskerville or Monington, they are likely to have been present too, especially Baskerville who was made Sheriff of Herefordshire by the Yorkists in 1460.

The Duke of York remained inactive in Dublin till September, when he finally returned, passing through Shrewsbury, Ludlow and Hereford. Waurin says that at Ludlow the 'seigneurs du pays de galles' (lords of Wales), presumably meaning Herbert, Vaughan,

Devereux and their allies, urged York to take the throne because of his descent from Lionel, Duke of Clarence. This meant asserting the Mortimer claim: 'the people on the Marches of Wales,' wrote the Tudor chronicler Edward Hall, 'above measure favoured the lineage of the Lord Mortimer.' Herbert had been York's councillor for many years and having turned his coat yet again after Northampton, he may well have thought that the policy of the Neville earls and Edward, of using Henry VI as a puppet king under Yorkist control, did not go far enough. The queen would never forgive Herbert for his apostacy, and he, a ruthless and ambitious man, may have thought it in his best interest to help York to the throne. If so, he misjudged the mood of the earls and, according to Waurin, of the Londoners too.

Richard of York made a regal progress to London, where he demanded the throne as his right, to the embarrassment of Warwick, Salisbury, Edward and the Archbishop of Canterbury. They all knew that the peers were very reluctant to abjure their oaths of allegiance to the poor imbecile king. Parliament arranged an impractical compromise called the Act of Accord, whereby York was content to become Henry's heir, so that Henry had to disinherit his own son. By a bitter irony Henry had inherited his French throne from his mad grandfather Charles VI, who had treated his own heir, the future Charles VII, in the same unnatural way.

Whilst the indomitable queen was at liberty she could not accept the grim verdict of Northampton as final. She fled with her son to Wales, and after a dangerous journey reached Harlech. 'Thence hence,' says Gregory, 'she removed full privily unto the Lord Jasper, Lord and Earl of Pembroke,' most likely at Tenby or Pembroke. Tenby was Jasper's favourite castle but has no natural harbour, whilst Pembroke is securely sited on a branch of Milford Haven. This magnificent harbour is ideally placed for anyone whose plans necessitate simultaneous access to France, Ireland or Scotland. It had been Strongbow's base for his Irish expedition in 1169. A French army had landed there in 1405 to help Owain Glyn Dwr. Jasper and Henry Tudor were to arrive there with another French army in 1485 on their way to Bosworth, and for the moment no other port could have suited the queen and Jasper better.

There can therefore be little reasonable doubt that the queen and Jasper, her brother-in-law and distant cousin, planned to use Pembroke as the base for an attack on Wigmore and Ludlow. Jasper would be in command; his partner would be James Butler, Earl of Wiltshire and Ormond. Orders probably reached Wiltshire while he was in Holland to obtain troops from the King of France and from the Duke of Brittany, and to take them to Pembroke, where they were to be joined by some of his Irish clansmen. The Estates General, Brittany's parliament, met at Vannes in September 1460, when Lancastrian envoys could well have presented Duke Francis II and his council with a request for troops. We do not know how it was arranged. The only reference to these foreign troops is in *A Short English Chronicle* (better perhaps called Gairdner's Chronicle after its editor), but this evidence may be accepted, as Margaret of Anjou was to make regular use of French troops in her future campaigns.

The main Lancastrian offensive, about which much more is known, was to be from the north. In mid-October the queen sailed to Scotland, probably from Pembroke, to negotiate with Queen Mary of Guelders, the Dutch widow of James II of Scotland who had been accidentally killed in August, whilst besieging Roxburgh Castle. Margaret's proposal to cede Roxburgh and Berwick in exchange for Scottish troops was accepted. In this way the French Queen of England can be seen reviving the 'Auld Alliance' between Scotland and France, now using Scottish and French help to restore the weak Lancastrian regime; this was preferable from the French viewpoint to the bellicose Yorkists, who were likely to revive the Plantagenet claim to the throne of France. Meanwhile, Margaret had ordered the Duke of Somerset and the Earl of Devon to bring reinforcements from the west country, which joined her already formidable northern army at Hull, early in December 1460.

The Duke of York was once again Protector, and as the queen and her lords were technically rebels, he very rashly decided to move against them. The systematic ravaging of York's and Salisbury's lands in the West Riding of Yorkshire may well have deliberately been intended to hand the choleric duke a challenge which he and Salisbury could not ignore. Allowing themselves to be lured into Yorkshire they prepared to march north, leaving Warwick in charge of the king, and sending Edward to the Welsh Marches. At the tragic end of his career one wonders whether Richard of York was in his right mind, for his march into Yorkshire was foolhardy to say the least. He and Salisbury spent Christmas at Sandal Castle, near Wakefield. The queen was still in Scotland, but Somerset, Northumberland and Trollope moved in on them with overwhelming force and on 30 December York, Rutland and most of their army were slaughtered, whilst Salisbury was beheaded next day. Their heads, York's wearing a paper crown, adorned the Micklegate Bar at York.

Edward, Earl of March

Rose and fetterlock, Yorkist badges

Presumably the Duke of York and his heir had held very full and serious discussions before they went their separate ways: York to his death at Wakefield, and Edward on his first independent command, for their parting might easily prove final. They may well have considered Edward's position if York was slain, in which case under the Act of Accord Edward would become heir to the throne. Since, however, the queen and her nobles were hardly likely to recognise the Act, it was really a dead letter. Taking the throne by force might become the only solution. One cannot believe that such a possibility was not considered, especially as it had been York's original aim.

Edward was not yet nineteen; contemporary opinion was unanimous about his good looks. Physically, his grandson Henry VIII was to be equally impressive. Edward was unusually tall, strong and athletic; he was open, charming, friendly and generous – a more attractive character than Henry VIII was to show. He also had a very good head for business, and was much more industrious than has been supposed. Finally, he possessed great courage, audacity, determination and military skill; although his character deteriorated in later life, no prince of the Plantagenet line was better equipped for kingship. As Earl of March he was heir to the Mortimers, a name which was more important in the Marches than Plantagenet, and as a young boy he had spent several years at Ludlow with his brother Edmund, Earl of Rutland. Knowing the Ludlow district and its people well, he was thus admirably prepared for the first great test of his career. No doubt he was already well acquainted with the Devereux, Herberts and Vaughans; whilst there is evidence of a boyhood squabble with Richard Croft and his brother, this in no way prejudiced their future relations. He was also known as Edward of Rouen, where he was born on 28 April 1442.

As king, Edward's understanding of his duties suggests diligent attention to the practical management of the landed estates of his great earldom during those years at Ludlow. Much time was probably spent with stewards, receivers and bailiffs, not only at Ludlow and Wigmore, but also at Usk, Montgomery, New Radnor and Crickhowell. Carefree days would have been passed hunting over Bringewood Chase, the hills towards Aymestrey, and Deerfold Forest to the west of Wigmore, whose name may be derived from the Welsh *gwig mawr*, or great forest, – the tangled hills, steep valleys and oak woods between Wigmore, Lingen and Shobdon which Edward must have known and enjoyed. These activities would have developed a natural eye for country, and even more important, a cordial relationship with hunters, foresters and other ordinary folk. Edward was always an affable and approachable man, who liked to cultivate admiration, so he is unlikely to have despised the opinions of men who knew the country far better than he did.

Edward would also have been in constant touch with the officers in charge of Ludlow and Wigmore Castles, 'men of war' such as were to be with him at Mortimer's Cross. These soldiers had experience in France, Ireland, Wales and perhaps the Scottish Marches; they also inherited centuries of military tradition in the defence of the middle March: knowledge of its geography, routes into Wales, and where to meet an advancing enemy on the most favourable terms. With this they no doubt included a well-tried system of political and military intelligence. It may also be assumed that Edward had plenty of opportunity to study the country during his visits to the other Mortimer castles. No doubt Edward's great height and strength made him an apt pupil for those men-at-arms who taught him how to use the sword, lance and axe; his prowess on the battlefield was an important part of his reputation as a king and war leader.

After his father's departure for the north, Edward went to the Marches probably accompanied by Devereux, Herbert and other Marchmen, for if Waurin is right in saying that they encouraged York to demand the crown, it is likely that they had gone to London with York. Also, since they were to be with Edward at Mortimer's Cross, the following men probably accompanied him too: the young Lord Audley, Humphrey Stafford and a Norfolk baron, Lord Fitzwater. Audley had been with the king at Ludford Bridge, but both he and Humphrey Stafford had been captured at Calais and had joined the Yorkist cause. It seems certain that they spent Christmas at Shrewsbury, as several chroniclers say, one giving their accommodation as a friary, and not at Gloucester as stated in Gairdner's Chronicle, for Gloucester was well outside Edward's home area. This point is important, as it bears on his likely intentions, for it has been assumed that his mission was to recruit troops to help his father. On the other hand, York's record was by now so disastrous that little good may have been expected of his northern enterprise, and its ruinous outcome may well have confirmed the worst fears of Edward and Warwick. It may reasonably be inferred that Edward and his marcher councillors were unanimous in thinking that never again must the Marches, the cornerstone of Yorkist power, be exposed to such a disaster as Ludford, and that the immediate threat was from Jasper Tudor and his powerful affinity in south-west Wales. Until this threat was dealt with there could be no question of leaving the Marches unguarded, and even had he wished to do so, Edward could hardly have persuaded the Marchmen to follow him.

If this reasoning is correct, the Yorkists would already have been keeping a close watch on Jasper Tudor. They had a listening post far to the west at Kidwelly, home of the Yorkist family of Dwnn. Later, Jasper was to put most of the blame for his defeat on 'traitors March, Herbert and Dwnns', which suggests that John Dwnn, head of the family, was present at Mortimer's Cross.

The news of Wakefield and of the deaths of his father and brother must have caused Edward the greatest shock and grief, but the two differing chronicle accounts need careful comparison. Gairdner's Chronicle is alone in saying that Edward was at Gloucester, and goes on to record that, hearing that the queen's northern army was on its way south, Edward sent for help to various shires and soon had 30,000 good men coming to his aid. This account was repeated by Edward Hall in 1548, so has tended to be accepted down to our own day. In fact there is no real evidence that Edward did raise an army of anything like that size. After Mortimer's Cross, Warwick sent him orders to recruit throughout the western shires from Stafford to Dorset, which may explain the rumour, but by then the queen had at last joined her army and begun her advance on London; Warwick's order reflected his alarm. There are no signs that Edward obeyed him.

Despite his grief, Edward seems to have kept a very cool head, as he always did at times of danger. There was no precipitate move by the Yorkists at Shrewsbury in response to Wakefield; nor did anything dramatic happen until Mortimer's Cross. Gairdner's Chronicle implies that the news of Jasper's advance was a bolt from the blue, preventing the supposed punitive expedition into Yorkshire. No doubt Edward wanted to avenge his father's death, but to launch a second foolhardy assault on the queen's great northern army was not the way to do it. Jasper's advance was expected, and he must be dealt with first.

The Battle of Mortimer's Cross

Roses, symbols of the House of York

The defeat of Jasper Tudor was Edward's first priority, which is borne out by the terse account in the *Brut Chronicle*, followed almost verbatim by others: 'And this time, the earl of March being in Shrewsbury, hearing the death of his father, desired assistance and aid of the town for to avenge his father's death; and from thence went to Wales, where, at Candlemas after, he had a battle at Mortimer's Cross against the earls of Pembroke and Wiltshire.'

Several other slightly earlier accounts place the battle near Wigmore. *An English Chronicle*, also known after its editor as Davies's Chronicle, says, 'beside Wigmore in Wales.' The tradition in the *Brut*

Chronicle fits the political and military realities of the situation better than does the one which comes via Hall from Gairdner's Chronicle, for there is absolutely no evidence of Edward dashing back from Gloucester in the nick of time to defend Wigmore from Jasper.

It looks as if Edward found little support in Shrewsbury, and moved on to Wigmore, probably quite soon after hearing the news of Wakefield. As this news took only three days to reach London, arriving there on 2 January, it could have been known in Shrewsbury even sooner, for whilst it is 182 miles from Wakefield to London, it is only 104 to Shrewsbury. The battle of Mortimer's Cross was over a month in the future, and the indications are that this month's delay put time very much on the side of Edward and his friends. They could sit and wait in comfort at Ludlow and Wigmore where they had plenty of provisions, from where they could watch the situation develop, and plan to meet the enemy on ground of their own choice, when he should come. With these advantages, Edward did not have the expense of paying and feeding a large army, as the formidable group of men who now came to his aid were mostly from the southern Marches and could quickly come with their retainers as soon as they were needed.

Jasper Tudor would not have begun his march until Wiltshire and the foreign contingents had arrived. We do not know whether they all came together, but it seems most likely that they did and that Wiltshire was with them. It is thought unlikely by Dr. Thomas, Jasper's biographer, that he had also been overseas and returned with them, as Gairdner's Chronicle says. A winter voyage could easily have been delayed by bad weather, and it looks as if Wiltshire was very late arriving. This would explain the long interval between Wakefield and Mortimer's Cross, for Jasper would hardly have kept the foreigners kicking their heels for so long. Invasion forces at this time tended to march as soon as possible after landing; in 1485 the Tudors covered the 130 miles from Milford Haven to Shrewsbury in eight days, with the battle of Bosworth only a week later.

While the foreigners were recovering from their seasickness, perhaps, Jasper would have been gathering his Pembroke retainers and their men, and ordering those in Carmarthen and Gower to meet his army at Carmarthen or Llandovery. These proceedings could well have attracted the attention of Edward's agents, such as the Dwnns at Kidwelly, giving him ample warning. We do not know how well each side was informed of the other's movements. Perhaps the news of Wiltshire's disembarkation at Pembroke with the foreign mercenaries was unexpected, but it could hardly have taken place before about 20 January. The march of about 110 miles from Pembroke to Mortimer's Cross would have taken at least a week, the battle being on 3 February. It therefore seems probable that Jasper had to endure a maddening delay of about three weeks after hearing of Wakefield, and before his principal ally turned up with reinforcements. The moral impetus would have been reduced, and time would have become more vital than ever.

After completing the first stage up the Towy valley to Llandovery, the route taken would beyond reasonable doubt have been over to the Usk valley at Trecastle, 850 feet above sea level, and then through Brecon, a friendly town belonging to the late Duke of Buckingham. From there into Herefordshire, along the north bank of the Wye from Glasbury, the way is easy, as it is onward to Leominster past Sarnesfield and Weobley. Jasper was making a midwinter march, well outside the normal campaigning season; he required food for some thousands of troops and followers, and forage for hundreds of horses. These considerations, together with the season and the possibility of severe cold and even blizzards, really rule out the alternative route from Llandovery which crosses the Sugarloaf Pass at 950 feet, goes through sparsely populated country around Builth and New Radnor, which belonged to Warwick and York respectively, and between which lies the 1,250 feet pass at Forest Inn. There are two further reasons against this route, and in favour of the other. First, Jasper had every possible reason for haste. Secondly, the Brecon route, not the Builth one, gives the approach to Mortimer's Cross where the battle was to take place.

Meanwhile Edward and his staff were planning to fight on their own ground and could therefore choose the site of the battle; in 1314, King Robert Bruce had a similar advantage in choosing Bannockburn on the road which King Edward II would have to take if he was to relieve the English garrison at Stirling. A Lancastrian attack on Wigmore and Ludlow appears to have been certain; the Yorkists may have had positive information to that effect. In that case, and if the enemy advanced from the direction of Brecon, the ideal meeting-place would be Mortimer's Cross.

Geographically the site is a remarkable one. Two valleys, cutting through the limestone escarpment whose dip slope rises gently from the north Herefordshire plain, meet there at right angles. The western one, with a farm called Covenhope at its summit, may have been an interglacial course of the River Lugg, the Afon Llugwy, the brilliant, shining river which enters the eastern valley a mile to the north at Aymestrey. It then runs east of and parallel to the Roman road, which at Mortimer's Cross intersects the newer road from Ludlow to Presteigne and Central Wales, for the direct modern road leading west up the cutting to Shobdon may date only from the eighteenth century.

A short way south of this later crossroads, the main road veers left towards Kingsland, while the Roman road continues as a straight, narrow lane, and indeed is called Hereford Lane, showing that it was there before the turnpikes were built. Here tradition has left two signposts: the cottage called Blue Mantle, still the title of a royal pursuivant or herald, and the rotten stump of the once mighty Battle Oak. This marks a frontage of about five hundred yards, whilst to the left is the Lugg, and to the right a steep, rising bank which forms the west side of the Covenhope valley. It looks a most promising position for a battle such as the Yorkists were probably planning, with well protected flanks, and on their right steep slopes which were almost certainly wooded in those days, and admirably suited for archers to deliver a storm of arrows against the left flank of an enemy force advancing from the south. Guns could also have been placed here, if any were available after the systematic disarming of the Yorkist castles which the master of the ordnance, John Judde, had been commissioned to carry out after Ludford.

The first modern historian to have understood the defensive merits of Mortimer's Cross seems to have been Flavell Edmunds, whose printed pamphlet is dated 1851; the plan in this booklet is based on his. He may be imitating an earlier plan, for certainly he used previous ideas in his paper. He was not concerned about the vital question of the approach march, but in a recent biography of

Edward IV, Mary Clive saw that the Brecon route was the most likely. Another Victorian writer, W. S. Symonds, wrote a wildly fanciful novel called *Malvern Chase*, in which he favoured the view that Jasper Tudor's army came from the west. This was also the opinion of a much more important writer, Howell Evans, whose plan shows that he cannot have visited the place, though his book is a scholarly study, containing a full account of Ludford and Mortimer's Cross. Four writers on battlefields during the last twenty years reproduce Evans's view of the approach route, showing the Yorkists waiting with their backs to the Lugg. Nothing that we know of Edward, the boldest and most aggressive commander of his day, or of his experienced captains suggests that they would have behaved in such a supine manner. They knew the country, and if the enemy had really been coming from the west, they would have marched out to meet him, for there are several good positions between Byton Hand and Forest Inn. At Byton the invader could have been caught between a steep hill and a bog. Edward had been at both Ludford and Northampton, where on each occasion the defenders had been beaten with their backs to a river, and he was not likely to risk disaster in a position totally unsuited to resisting an advance from the west, but ideal for facing an enemy coming from the south. It seems clear that the Yorkists chose to wait at Mortimer's Cross for an enemy known to be coming from Pembroke through Brecon towards Wigmore. It is curious that none of the authors seem to have felt the need for refreshment when visiting the battlefield, for they would have seen at the Mortimer's Cross Inn a beautifully drawn plan based on Edmunds's theory, as is also the excellent display at Hereford City Museum.

Samuel Daniel was a contemporary of Shakespeare, and author of an epic poem on the Wars of the Roses. As he was tutor to the descendants of William Herbert he could have picked up some oral tradition, and compares the 'young March' to a 'Libyan lion', who rushes out on his enemies from his den. If this is a true comparison, it bears out what has been suggested about the strategy of the campaign, and points to the tactics used when battle was joined.

Both armies were much smaller than at Ludford, where Henry VI had been followed by many great magnates with their retinues. At

Mortimer's Cross, the only great Yorkist magnate was Edward himself, so that his army consisted almost entirely of men from the southern Marches, as can be seen from William Worcester's list of his retainers. All the Marchmen except Walter Devereux had avoided York's muster in 1459, but in 1456 several had followed Herbert and Devereux into South Wales. On that occasion the Yorkist army had been about 2,000 strong, and the one which now came to fight for the Earl of March was probably very similar in size and personnel. William and Richard Herbert, Walter Devereux, John Lingen, Richard Croft, Roger Vaughan were all there, also Lord Grey of Wilton near Ross-on-Wye. Lord Audley, Lord Fitzwater and Humphrey Stafford have been mentioned as having probably come with Edward from London; Audley and Fitzwater both had manors in Herefordshire. All but one of the other fifteen names seem to be those of Herefordshire men. The exception, Walter Mytton, 'a man of the war of France,' came from a Shropshire family. Other French veterans were John Milewater whose father was one of York's receivers, and Philip Vaughan of Hay, 'the most noble esquire of lances among all the rest.' Other professional soldiers were Henry ap Gruffydd, Mr. Harper of Wellington, Richard Hakluyt, and William of Knill. Of the senior officers, certainly Herbert and probably Croft and others had military experience, giving the general impression of a tough, cohesive body of men who knew what they were about. It has been suggested that John Dwnn, James Baskerville and Thomas Monington were very likely there too. Another is Richard Croft the younger, brother of his namesake – a common if confusing family custom in those days. Thomas Vaughan of Hergest was as committed to the cause as his brother Roger, and his omission is surprising; *Malvern Chase* is wrong, as so often, in calling him a Lancastrian.

Jasper's army comprised the retinues of two magnates, but Wiltshire seems only to have brought an uncertain number of Irish, French and Bretons. The Irish were no doubt valiant but ill-armed; we know nothing of the others. Wiltshire's courage was more than doubtful. The army may have been as large as Edward's or bigger, but its men spoke five different languages, so it was much less cohesive. Jasper was certainly a brave, tenacious and resourceful man, without whose tireless labours Henry Tudor would never have become king in 1485, and his Welshmen were probably his best troops. With him were his already elderly father Owen, who had married Henry V's French widow, Sir Thomas Perot, and various esquires of Gower and Carmarthen, including two sons of Gruffydd ap Nicholas. Probably the Scudamores could show more military experience, for Sir John and Sir William may both have been at Agincourt, whilst there is some doubt as to whether Owen Tudor had been there. They and Sir John's sons came with thirty retainers. Others included the Hereford lawyer Thomas Fitzharry and an Englishman, John Throckmorton of Tewkesbury, another accomplice of William Herbert in the 1456 invasion of South Wales, who had joined the court party.

This polyglot force had to march over 100 miles, in winter and doubtless on short rations, through a country totally strange to many of them, and in a cause equally obscure. It is hard to see how their morale could have been anything like as good as that of their enemies, who were on their own ground, well fed and rested, and very clear about their business. The Yorkists also had time to prepare their bivouacs with plenty of firewood, an important advantage; not only was it winter, but the phenomenon of the Three Suns, or parhelion, suggests that the weather was very cold indeed, which would have increased the misery of the invaders. To emphasise the fact that the Yorkists were very much the 'home side', it is worth pointing out that the lands of two of their leaders lay immediately beyond the battlefield – Richard Croft and John Lingen both survived into the next century and were buried at Croft and Aymestrey Churches. They and their men had every incentive to fight hard.

The best that can be done, between the battles of Northampton and Mortimer's Cross, is to offer what seems with the limited evidence available to be the likeliest course of events. In January 1461 the Yorkists were probably collecting their army around Wigmore and Ludlow, to meet an attack which Jasper Tudor was expected to make on Wigmore. If his primary objective proved to be Ludlow, they could easily move their troops to Ludford to meet him, even though this was a less suitable site than Mortimer's Cross. However,

Gregory tells us that Edward mustered his army at Wigmarsh, near Hereford East, where the battle was fought. Hall also says Hereford East; perhaps the expression distinguishes the cathedral city from Haverfordwest in Pembrokeshire. In fact Mortimer's Cross is seventeen miles from Hereford. Gregory seems understandably to have confused Wigmore and Wigmarsh, which is an old alternative name for Widemarsh, outside the north gates of Hereford. Maybe the Yorkist army camped there after Mortimer's Cross because Gregory learned many interesting details, very probably from Yorkist soldiers who came to London for Edward's king-making; in those days a Londoner may have found the Herefordshire dialect very puzzling. Another error is that of John Speed, who placed the battle near Little Hereford, between Ludlow and Tenbury Wells, in his well known 1610 map of Herefordshire.

The first mention of the battle is in an Italian diplomatic paper. On 11 March the Milanese ambassador to the court of France, Prospero Camulio, wrote from Paris to tell Francesco Sforza that on 3 February the Earl of March had defeated the Earls of Pembroke and Wiltshire. In the interval there had been a period of mounting panic with the approach of the queen's army, and her victory over Warwick on 17 February at the second battle of St. Albans. It was very difficult, even for the Italian community in London, to know exactly what the unpredictable northern barbarians were doing, and the storm-swept Channel made news gathering even harder. All this helps us to see why the battle of Mortimer's Cross has been so obscure ever since.

Worcester recalls that the battle was fought on St. Blaise's Day, Tuesday 3 February, 1461. Benet's Chronicle, found in Dublin in 1962 agrees, as does the very authoritative Davies's Chronicle:

'The 3rd. day of February the same year, Edward the noble Earl of March fought with the Welshmen beside Wigmore in Wales, whose captains were the Earl of Pembroke and the Earl of Wiltshire, that would finally have destroyed the said Earl of March.

'And the Monday before the day of battle, that is to say, in the feast of Purification of our blessed lady (Candlemas) about 10 at clock before noon, were seen 3 suns in the firmament shining full clear, whereof the people had great marvel, and thereof were aghast. The noble Earl Edward them comforted and said. "Be of good comfort and dread not; this is a good sign, for these three suns betoken the Father, the Son and the Holy Ghost, and therefore let us have a good heart, and in the name of Almighty God go we against our enemies." And so by His Grace, he had the victory of his enemies, and put the 2 earls to flight, and slew of the Welshmen to the number of 4,000.

'After this discomfiture he came to London, the 28th. day of the month abovesaid, and anon fell unto him people innumerable, ready for to go with him into the north, to venge the death of the noble Duke Richard his father.'

Several comments are needed. First, the Yorkist chronicler agrees most emphatically with Worcester and Camulio about the date, which seems to have become accepted shortly afterwards as Candlemas, 2 February, because this date is that of one of the very great feast days of the Church, more memorable than St. Blaise – patron saint of wool combers, the comb being the instrument of his martyrdom. Secondly, the impression is that the Yorkists were waiting in order of battle at Mortimer's Cross when the famous parhelion was seen, in which case the enemy probably arrived that afternoon. Had the enemy gone on to Leominster, an attack on Ludlow was indicated, but the Yorkists would have had time to march to Ludford via Richard's Castle. Finally, the writer does not name the battle, unlike Blore Heath, an equally obscure place. Gregory is one of the first writers to refer to 'Mortimer his Cross'. It is said that one of the Mortimers erected a cross here in earlier times, and in any case, Gregory is likely to mean a wayside cross rather than a crossroads which probably did not exist at that time. On the Monument a mile away, Edward is significantly, if incorrectly, given the surname of Mortimer.

It seems that, on the morning of St. Blaise's Day, and as soon as men were more or less thawed out after their freezing bivouacs, the Lancastrian army formed up at its camp, which probably consisted of the baggage wagons chained into a circle. This may have been near the Monument which is a mile from the Battle Oak, perhaps on the Great West field where there is an old cottage called Battle Acre. A farm worker told Richard Brooke, author of a mid-nineteenth century book on battlefields, that he had found many metal objects hereabouts: bridle bits, stirrups, iron fragments and long pieces of iron on both sides of the turnpike road.

Deploying a polyglot, ill-disciplined force into the customary 'battles' (battalions) of vanguard, centre and rearguard must have been very difficult. Then came the advance over open fields. We must try and imagine the scene: disorderly ranks of men, probably no two of whom were dressed and armed alike. The motley appearance of the mediaeval army emerges vividly from the inspections carried out in that period by the Duke of Brittany of the Breton noblesse, an impoverished class akin to the Anglo-Welsh gentry, many of whom were considerably wealthier. The Bretons' arms and armour left much to be desired. Very few had full plate armour, which was very expensive; the best coming from Milan or Germany. Most had salades, the favourite helmet of the period, brigandines or quilted mail coats, swords and shields, guisarmes or bills, and daggers. Too many had no gauntlets, without which a man-at-arms could easily be disabled in close combat. Two or three armed retainers apiece were all that most could afford.

Jasper probably had most of his archers in front, but it is likely that Herefordshire and Gwent, the original home of the longbow, could provide Edward with far more archers than were available to his enemy. We do have one definite detail, which is that the Irish were in the van, information which is provided by an Elizabethan poem called *The Miseries of Queen Margaret* by Michael Drayton, and which seems to be the only reference to foreigners apart from Gairdner's Chronicle. If they actually entered the killing ground which was prepared for them to the south of Battle Oak, the likeliest consequence would have been withering flights of arrows from Yorkist archers lining the foot of the slope. In the Wars of the Roses, both sides usually had enough archers to make cavalry attacks impossible, so that most of the fighting took place on foot.

Edward's men were presumably drawn up in their 'battles' across the level ground between the steep bank and the river, with their archers to the fore as well as along the slopes, their centre near the Battle Oak and Blue Mantle. The men-at-arms, under such experienced officers, were probably picked household retainers, like those who, as Gregory noted, won the second battle of St. Albans. They would have carried halberts, brown bills, axes, swords or lead clubs and were 'harnessed men', with varying amounts of plate, chain mail and leather brigandines or 'jacks'.

Before a mediaeval battle, heralds often passed between the armies to attempt a peaceful settlement. Parleys had been held before Dartford, St. Albans and Northampton, but not, apparently, before Blore Heath, Ludford or Wakefield. After that grim slaughter, Edward may well have been in no mood to talk. There is, however, a vague tradition that his herald, Blue Mantle, was treacherously slain, which could account for the cottage near the Battle Oak bearing this title.

If the battle had indeed begun with an arrow storm beating against Jasper's left flank, the casualties could have been severe. The survivors would have moved away towards their centre, causing hopeless congestion, as the Yorkist men-at-arms charged. At Agincourt, the French had not only been surrounded, but so tightly pressed together that they could not defend themselves, even against lightly armed archers. Michael Drayton may have a unique description of the fighting, based perhaps on oral tradition:

'The Earl of Ormond ... came in the vanguard with his Irishmen,
    With darts and skains; those of the British blood,
    With shafts and gleaves, them seconding again,
    And as they fall still make their places good,
    That it amazed the Marchers to behold
    Men so ill-armed, upon their bows so bold.'

The desperate courage of the Irish owed nothing to their chief, who, according to Worcester, maintained his consistent reputation for cowardice by fleeing from the field at the start of the battle.

Edward, on the other hand, almost certainly fought as he always did in the midst of the battle, establishing his fame as a warrior as well as a skilful commander. He had already shown his quickness of wit in rallying his men when they were terrified by the apparition of the three suns; in Gairdner's Chronicle he at once knelt, prayed, and thanked God for the good omen.

Jasper was a man of undoubted courage, but if the situation was as grim as this, he could hardly do much to reverse it. The story repeated by Flavell Edmunds from an earlier Herefordshire historian who wrote *The Leominster Guide*, that Jasper led a successful charge and broke through the Yorkists right under the steep bank, seems unlikely, even more so that he could have pursued the enemy to Shobdon or Aymestrey. With their tactical advantages the Yorkists could have stopped such a move with arrow fire. It is much more likely that the Lancastrians were surrounded, pushed against the river bank, massacred and drowned. (This suggestion was made to the author by Dr. John Stephens, of Edinburgh University). A helmet of Italian type, called a barbute, was found in the Lugg at Lugwardine and can be seen in Hereford Museum. It might possibly have been lost at Mortimer's Cross, and washed slowly down river. Another possible but unprovable suggestion is that Edward put a small squadron of horse in ambush up the Buzzards Valley, with orders to take the enemy in the rear; he used this tactic at his last batttle, Tewkesbury.

There is reason to think, however, that fair numbers of the beaten army were able to escape from the main battle. Tradition suggests that some fled past Covenhope to the Lugg, only to be pursued and masacred near Kinsham; Slaughterhouse Covert and Bank may perhaps have been named after this. The evidence collected by Richard Brooke makes it highly likely that some sort of last stand was made near Battle Acre at the wagon laager. The survivors were, however, overwhelmed and perhaps it was there that the prisoners were taken, including Owen Tudor, who were later beheaded at Hereford. It is worth noticing that men of rank, protected by full plate armour, stood a better chance of surviving in hand-to-hand combat than common men, but the weight of their harness exhausted them sooner. They were also much more conspicuous. If the battle went against them, they might not reach their horses in time to escape. This was to be the Earl of Warwick's fate at the battle of Barnet.

Flavell Edmunds's narrative may have some bearing on this last stand; he picked the idea up from *The Leominster Guide* published in 1808, whose author was a local clergyman called Jonathan Price. According to the *Guide*, Jasper sent part of his army on to Leominster to reinforce Lancastrian troops who were already there, where they drove Yorkist detachments away. They were then themselves dislodged while the battle was raging at Mortimer's Cross and were driven out to Kingsland to join the routed main army, only to be involved in the final overthrow near the Monument. It is, however, very doubtful whether Jasper would have divided his army so deep inside hostile territory, as is the idea that there was a royalist garrsion in Leominster, an unwalled monastery town, far from the country controlled by Queen Margaret. It looks like romantic tradition, picked up or perhaps invented by Jonathan Price, who hardly inspires confidence; he tells a quite ridiculous story that Anne Neville, daughter of the Earl of Warwick and queen to Richard III, was kept by Edward IV as his mistress at Wigmore Castle. This is unlikely, as Anne was only born in 1456, and so only sixteen when she married Richard in 1472; nor would Warwick have allowed it! However, Yorkists from Leominster could well have joined in the final rout.

The figure of 4,000 slain seems excessive, as the armies probably each numbered only two or three thousand, but the tradition that it was a bloody battle may be accepted. After Ludford and Wakefield the Yorkists may have been in no mood to spare their foes who had invaded their country, no doubt plundering and committing atrocities. Yorkist casualties may have been light, for it is surely interesting that Worcester names none of Edward's companions as killed, though he says somewhat irrelevantly that Philip Vaughan was slain by a gunshot at the siege of Harlech, 'and no man of honour was slain there except him.' A bard laments the death of Watkin Vaughan, killed fighting in Herefordshire, but Watkin could be Walter Vaughan, whose murder in 1456 led his relation, William Herbert, to have several men unlawfully hanged in Hereford.

However this may be, there is a strong flavour of a Welsh clan battle about Mortimer's Cross, which has been suggested by Professor Griffiths in his *Tudor Dynasty*, with the victors bent on revenge. They spent three weeks in Hereford, where Owen Tudor, who had married Henry V's widowed queen, John Throckmorton, Henry Scudamore (son of Sir John), and other 'Welsh persons of the first distinction' were beheaded. Roger Vaughan led Owen to the block; the macabre scene at his death is well known from Gregory's description, surely derived from an eyewitness. Owen only realised that the end had come when he saw the axe and block, and when the red velvet collar of his doublet was torn off. The irony of so rough a pillow for 'the head that was wont to lie on Queen Katherine's lap' seems to have amused him, and 'he fully meekly took his end.' His severed head was then carefully washed, and the hair and beard combed by a 'mad woman', who placed it on the top step of the market cross, surrounded by over a hundred candles. Owen had fathered a future dynasty on Henry V's widowed queen; his indomitable son Jasper lived to take vengeance on Roger Vaughan, whom he caught in 1471, and to see his nephew Henry crowned king. Wiltshire also got away, but was caught and beheaded after Towton. Thomas Fitzharry, the sons of Gruffydd ap Nicholas and the other Scudamores slipped the net too; James was killed soon after, but his father, 'the most valiant of them all', and uncle both died in bed. Fighting patrols presumably chased the fleeing enemy into Wales to ensure that there was no further danger from that direction.

Edward IV

Portrait of a king, probably Edward III

It has been suggested that, at their final meeting, Edward and his father would have discussed the future of the Act of Accord, and what would happen if either of them should fall in battle. York was now dead, and Edward completely victorious over Jasper Tudor; his councillors were the very men who, according to Waurin, had only a few months earlier urged his father to take the crown. If this is true, they had presumably been giving Edward the same advice, to which Mortimer's Cross would have given added point. Did Herbert and Devereux now tell Edward to march on London and take the throne? We shall never know, though it seems very likely.

They were, however, certainly in no hurry to leave Hereford, even though news of the queen's advance from the north had doubtless reached them, together with Warwick's orders dated 12 February to raise the western shires. Warwick was still acting in King Henry's name, but not for long. Guarding the northern approaches to London, he drew up his army at St. Albans, where on 17 February he was caught by a surprise attack on the left flank. The queen, Somerset, Northumberland and Trollope won an overwhelming victory, and recaptured the puppet king. Badly mauled, outgeneralled and outwitted, Warwick retreated westwards. Edward, Herbert, Devereux and their army, swelled with fresh troops, left Hereford on hearing this news; so eager were the Marchmen to follow him now that Jasper was beaten, that most of them came at their own cost. Gregory, who tells us this, adds that Edward 'was full sore afeared' by the disaster of St. Albans coming on top of that of Wakefield, despite his own success; that he sorrowed also for his father and brother. When they met at Burford in the Cotswolds, however, Warwick assured him of the popular favour towards him, 'and by right to occupy the crown of England.' This does not exclude the argument that Edward and his councillors had already made this decision, which was clearly the only realistic course open to the Yorkists since Henry's defection to his own party.

A vivid impression of the panic in London at the coming of the queen's plundering hordes is given by members of the Italian community in the Milanese papers. Warwick had left the city quite exposed to the queen, but her rabble had begun to desert even before the second battle of St. Albans; she had no siege train, and despite the timidity of the leading citizens the temper of the ordinary Londoners was so hostile that she retreated. She had her king back, but never learned the lesson that a king who had lost London had lost England. The Yorkists, however, held London, but it was no thanks to Warwick, the 'shield of our defence.'

On the other hand, the day of 'Edward Earl of March, whose fame the earth shall spread', as the same ballad has it, had arrived. Public opinion was reflected in another ballad: 'had not the Rose of Rouen been, all England had been shent.' Lancastrian lawlessness was politically fatal; London thanked God for its deliverer, and the citizens were saying: 'let us walk in a new vineyard, and let us make a gay garden in the month of March, with this fair white rose and herb, the Earl of March.' He was proclaimed King Edward IV on 4 March, not 5 March as the Monument says; though no doubt Warwick stage-managed the proceedings with his usual skill, here he was no king-maker, and Edward was not his creature. The Londoners felt deserted by the unkingly Henry VI, and his heir by the Act of Accord, Richard Duke of York, was dead; the queen and all her affinity were abominated. This magnificent young man was the new Duke of York, victorious in battle and supported by the warriors of the Welsh Marches in force. He had proved, in the words soon to be used by Thomas Mallory in his Morte d'Arthur, that he was 'the rightwise King born of all England', who alone could draw the sword from the stone. This comparison could well have been made by members of an increasing literate generation, steeped in Arthurian romance. Moreover, London was the seat of majesty, as well as of commerce and government, and kings were crowned at Westminster with all the ceremonial hallowed by tradition.

Instead the coronation must be postponed. The young king and his supporters gathered a very large army, drawn from the Home Counties, the Midlands, East Anglia and the Welsh Marches. The quarrel of York and Lancaster was now a matter of the south seeking to impose its will on the north, not for the first nor the last time in our history. On 28 March the Yorkists forced the crossing of the River Aire at Ferrybridge, near Pontefract in Yorkshire, against fierce resistance; Lord Fitzwater was killed and Warwick wounded. Fitzwater's presence reinforces the view that those who had been with Edward at Mortimer's Cross were eager to see it through with him to the end. On the next day, Palm Sunday, Edward met the even larger host of Somerset and the northern lords near Towton, where about 50,000 men are believed to have fought for six hours in flurries of snow. The Lancastrians were defeated with hideous slaughter, and Edward was king indeed. His coronation followed on 28 June. The heir of York and Mortimer had secured the English throne and his favourite device became the Sun in Splendour, portent of victory at Mortimer's Cross.

Edward was generous to those who served him well. During his 'first reign', before Warwick's rebellion in 1469, he relied on Herbert, Devereux and Dwnn to overcome resistance in Wales, which was accomplished in 1464, though Harlech Castle held out till 1468. Knighthoods were conferred at different times on Devereux, Richard Herbert, Roger Vaughan, Baskerville, Croft, Lingen and Knill. Lucrative stewardships were given to John Harper, John Milewater and Thomas Vaughan. Richard Croft the elder added the manors of Leintwardine and Burford to Croft and was knighted in 1471 after the battle of Tewkesbury, which was fatal to the House of Lancaster. Richard the younger became parker at the royal manor of Woodstock, founding a new branch of the House of Croft, from which sprang William Croft the musician, (1678–1727).

William Herbert, described by a bard as Edward's 'master lock' in Wales, became Earl of Pembroke. He and Humphrey Stafford, now Earl of Devon, were defeated in 1469 by one of Warwick's northern captains at Edgecote, near Banbury. Nearly 200 Welsh gentlemen were killed on that disastrous day according to William Worcester. Richard Herbert and Thomas Vaughan fell fighting desperately, with others of the houses of Davy Gam and Dwnn. William Herbert, whose eminence in Wales had aroused Warwick's murderous jealousy, was beheaded at Northampton. Thomas Vaughan's magnificent tomb can be seen in Kington parish church.

'He that was the most king and noblest knight of the world, and most loved the fellowship of noble knights, ... might not these Englishmen hold them content with him.' Thomas Mallory is thought to have had Edward in mind, writing of Mordred's rebellion against King Arthur at the very time that Warwick was restoring Henry VI; but Edward returned from his brief exile in 1471, to triumph over all his enemies, and enjoy an unchallenged 'second reign.' While he lived, his formidable personality kept his court and nobles in awe, especially after 1478, when he finally had his treacherous brother Clarence put to death. His own sudden death in 1483 was followed by the controversial accession, and brief, troubled reign, of Richard III. Walter Devereux, now Lord Ferrers of Chartley, was among those who fell fighting for Richard at

Bosworth. There the Tudors reversed the verdict of Mortimer's Cross. The end of the House of York was a melancholy affair, but Edward's eldest daughter Elizabeth married Henry Tudor, and from them all our subsequent sovereigns are descended.

Y Ddraig goch – The Red Dragon

'The Dishonourable white dragon has triumphed,
But the red dragon will yet win the field.'
(Welsh bard Robin Ddu on the death of Owen Tudor whose grandson Henry was to carry the Red Dragon banner of Cadwallader to victory at Bosworth in 1485. Quoted from Evans's *Wales and the Wars of the Roses*).

This pedeſtal is erected to perpetuate the Memory of an obstinate, bloody, and deciſive battle fought near this Spot in the civil Wars between the ambitious Houſes of York and Lancaster, on the 2ⁿᵈ Day of February 1461 between the *Forces* of *Edward Mortimer* Earl of March, (afterwards *Edward* the *Fourth*) on the Side of York and thoſe of *Henry* the *Sixth*, on the Side of Lancaster.

The Kings Troops were commanded by *Jaſper* Earl of Pembroke, *Edward* commanded his own in Person and was victorious. The Slaughter was great on both Sides Four Thousand being left dead on the Field and many Welſh Perſons of the firſt diſtinction were taken Prisoners among whom was *Owen Tudor* (Great-Grandfather to *Henry* the *Eighth* and a Deſcendent of the illuſtrious *Cadwallader*) who was afterwards beheaded at Hereford

This was the deciſive Battle which fixed *Edward* the *Fourth* on the Throne of England who was proclaimed King in London on the Fifth of March following

Erected by Subſcription in the Year 1799

The Monument at Kingsland commemorating Mortimer's Cross (author)

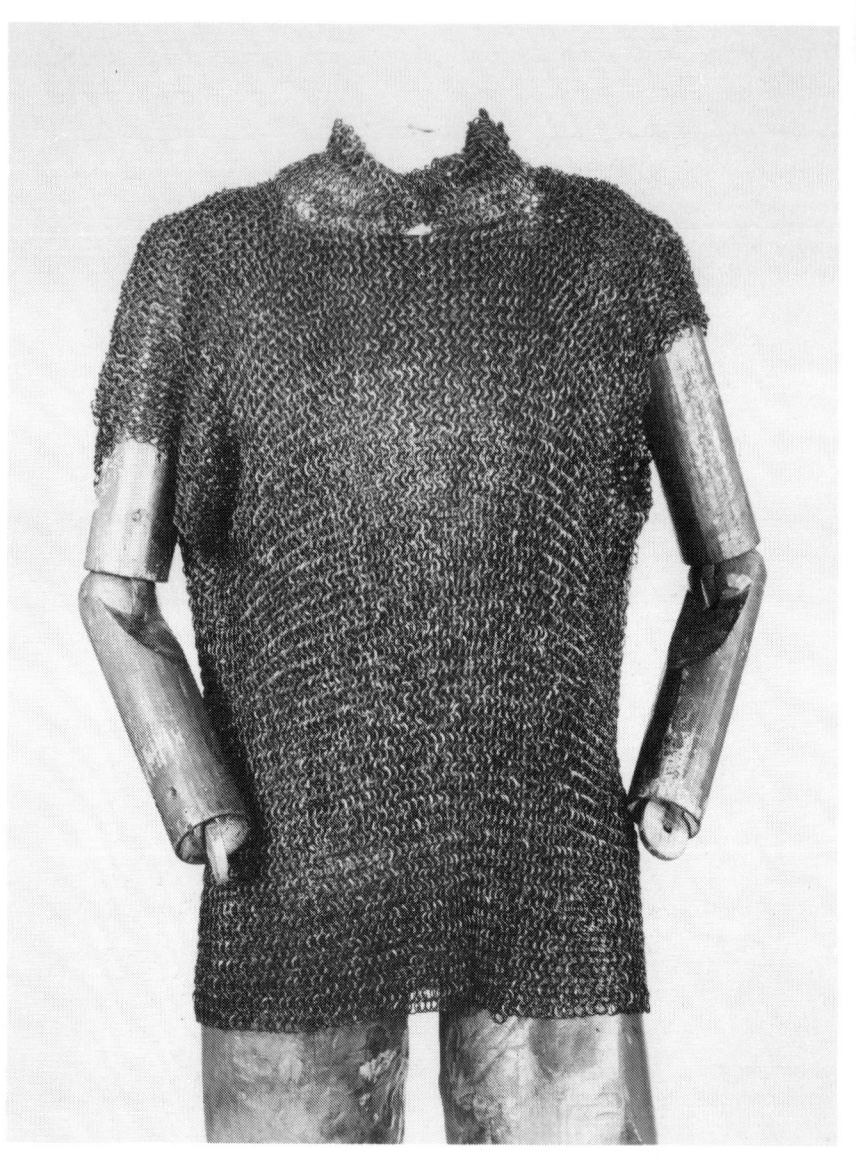

Mail shirt, 15th. century. Constructed of riveted rings of flat section, the shirt is hip-length, sleeveless with a standing collar of smaller rings than the rest. The front opening was fastened by a strap passing from the right where a brass rivet and washer remain to a brass buckle on the left.
(Courtesy of the Board and Trustees of the Royal Armouries)

Armour for man and horse in the German 'Gothic' style, late 15th. century. The surfaces of the plates are decorated with ripple-like flutes and some of the edges are cusped. The overall effect is slender, elongated and spiky. (Courtesy of The Board and Trustees of the Royal Armouries)

Incomplete armour in the 'Gothic' style composed of various pieces of the same period and fashion. It is of a type made in Italy for export to Germany and Western Europe. (Courtesy of the Board and Trustees of the Royal Armouries)

Billman of the period of the Wars of the Roses, in north Italian sallet (or salade) and brigandine, about 1470-80 with mail collar and sleeves. (Courtesy of the Board and Trustees of the Royal Armouries)

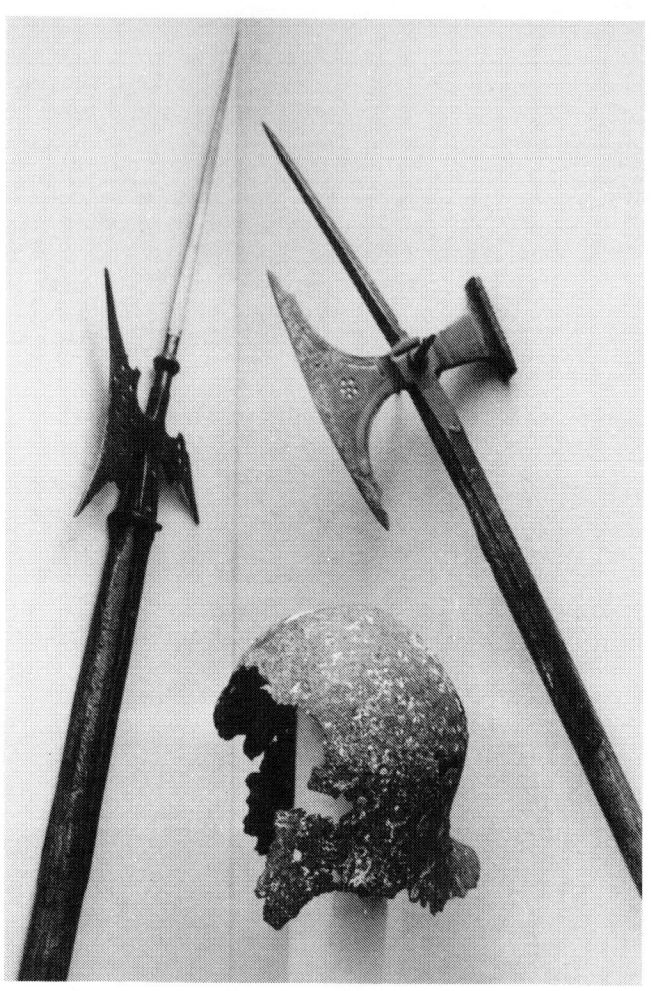

Armour in Hereford City Museum. The helmet is a barbute of a type which originated in Italy. It provided good all round protection with a T shaped gap for breathing and vision. It was found in the Lugg twelve miles downstream from Mortimer's Cross, and was perhaps lost in the Lancastrian flight or was washed down river from the battle site. The pole axes are late fifteenth or early sixteenth century, with spikes for thrusting and axe blades and hammerheads for breaking open armour. The shafts would have been 5 to 6 feet in length, with strips of iron running down from the balde to protect it from being cut off (Ray Lloyd)

The 'Boxted Bombard' perhaps English, 15th. century. Like other mediaeval iron guns of this size, it is built up of wrought iron strips bound together with iron hoops. The breech is forged solid. (Courtesy of The Board and Trustees of the Royal Armouries)

Wigmore Castle (author)

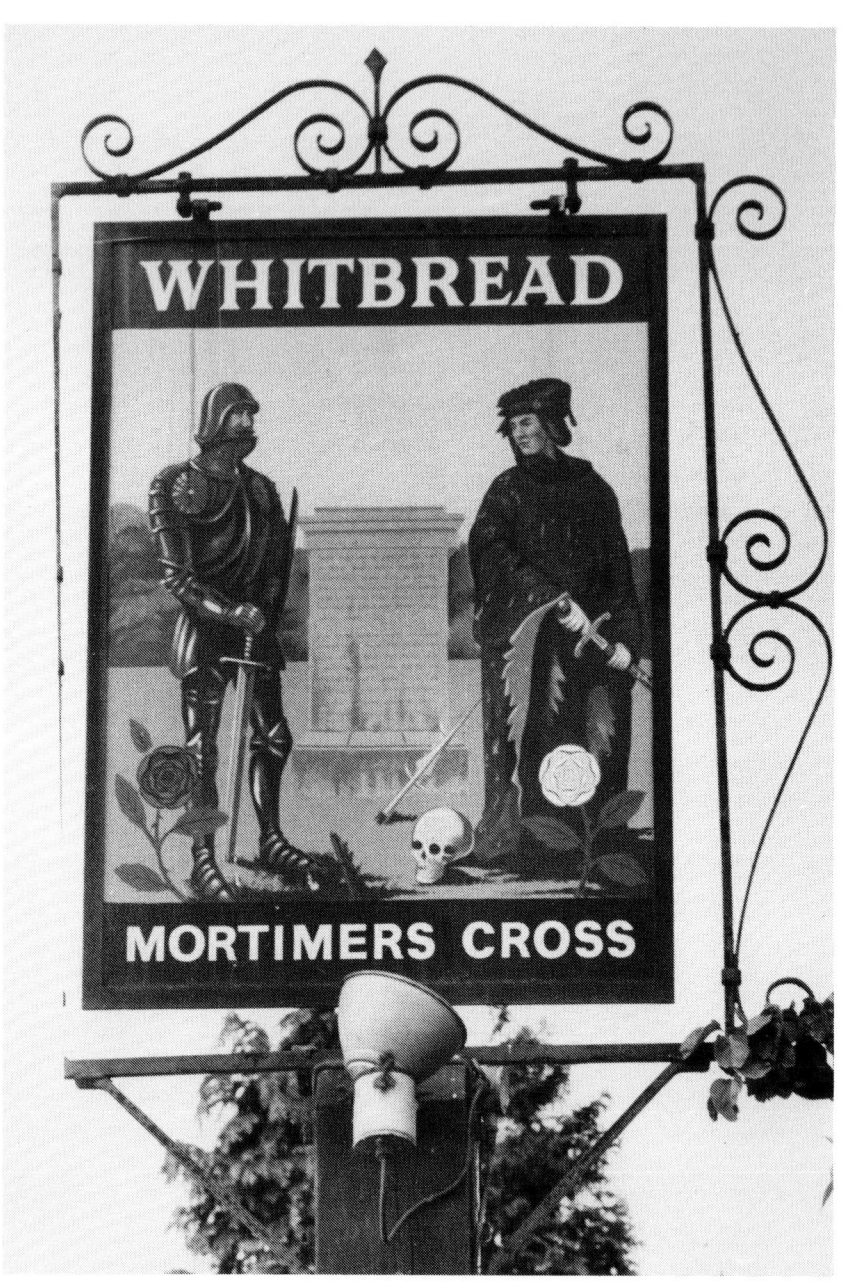

The Two Warriors, old sign at Mortimer's Cross Inn (author)

The Three Suns, old sign at Mortimer's Cross Inn (author)

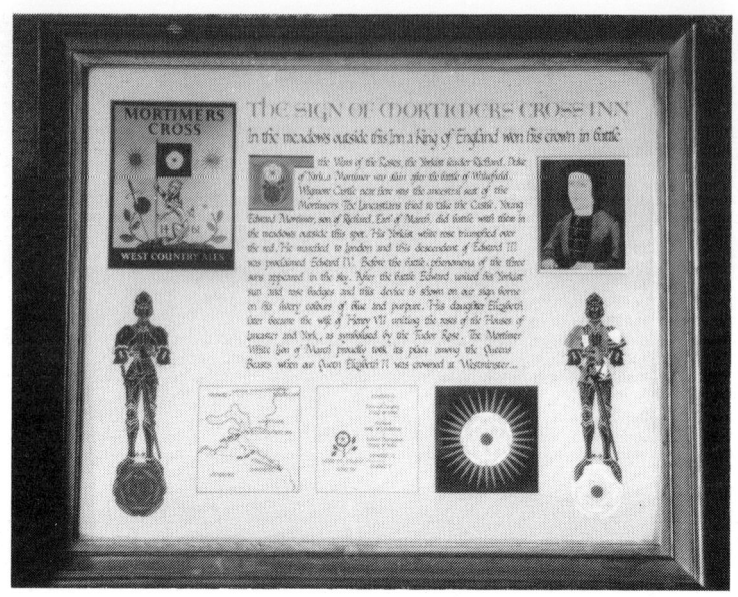

Picture in the bar, Mortimer's Cross Inn (Ben Corbett)

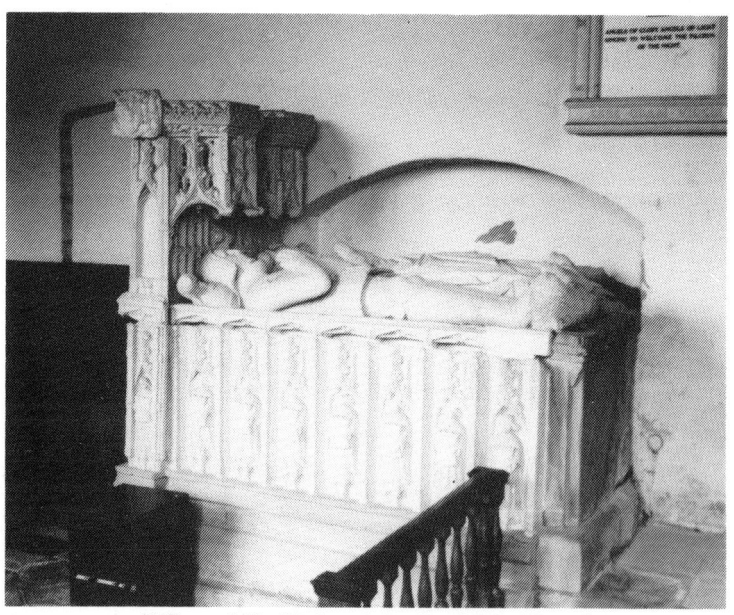

Effigy of Sir Richard Croft, Croft Church

Effigy of Thomas Vaughan of Hergest, Kington Church (Ben Corbett)

Aymestrey Church, where the Yorkists may have stabled some of their horses and equipment before the battle (author)

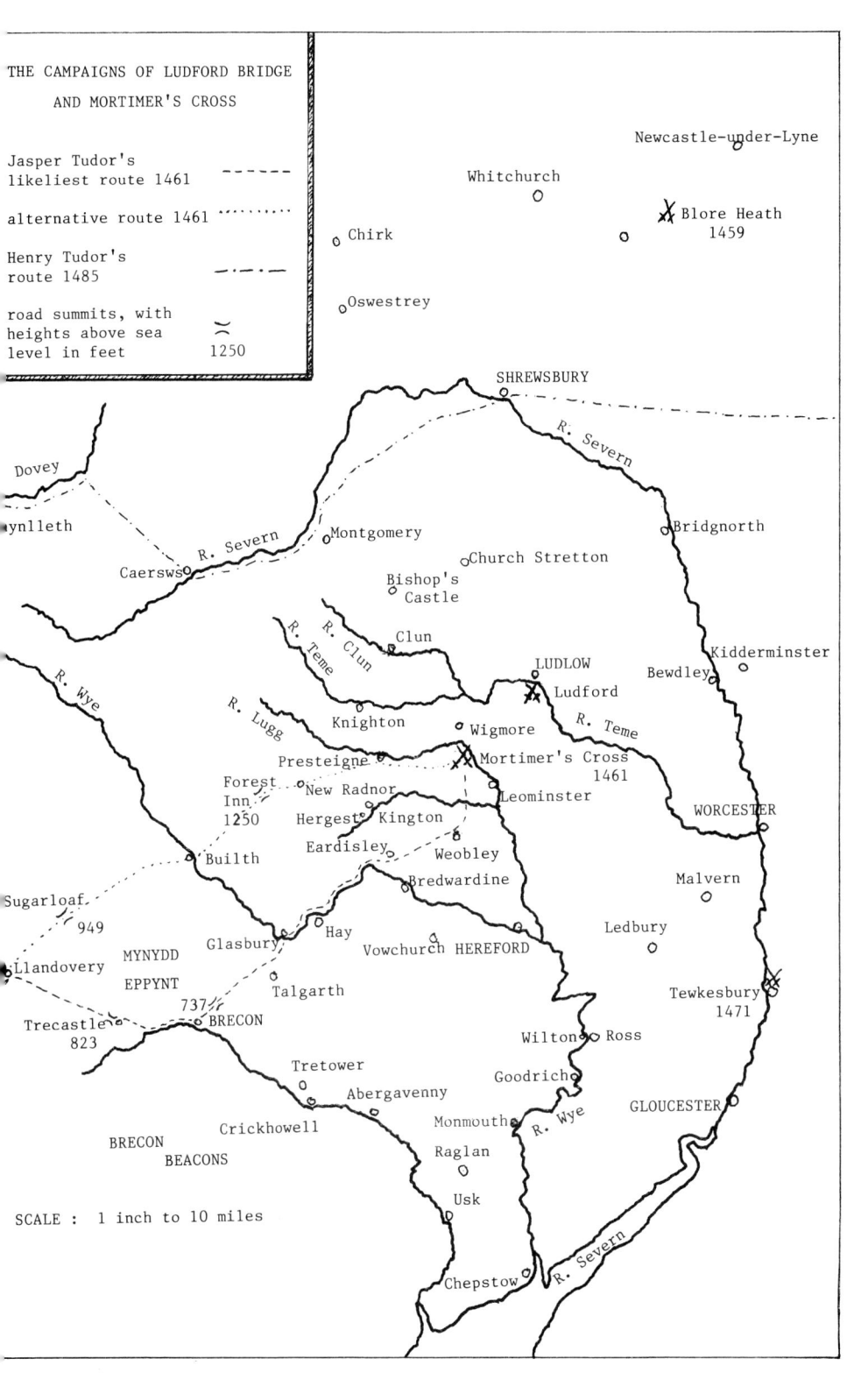

THE CAMPAIGNS OF LUDFORD BRIDGE AND MORTIMER'S CROSS

Jasper Tudor's likeliest route 1461   ------

alternative route 1461   ....

Henry Tudor's route 1485   —·—·—

road summits, with heights above sea level in feet   ~ 1250

SCALE : 1 inch to 10 miles

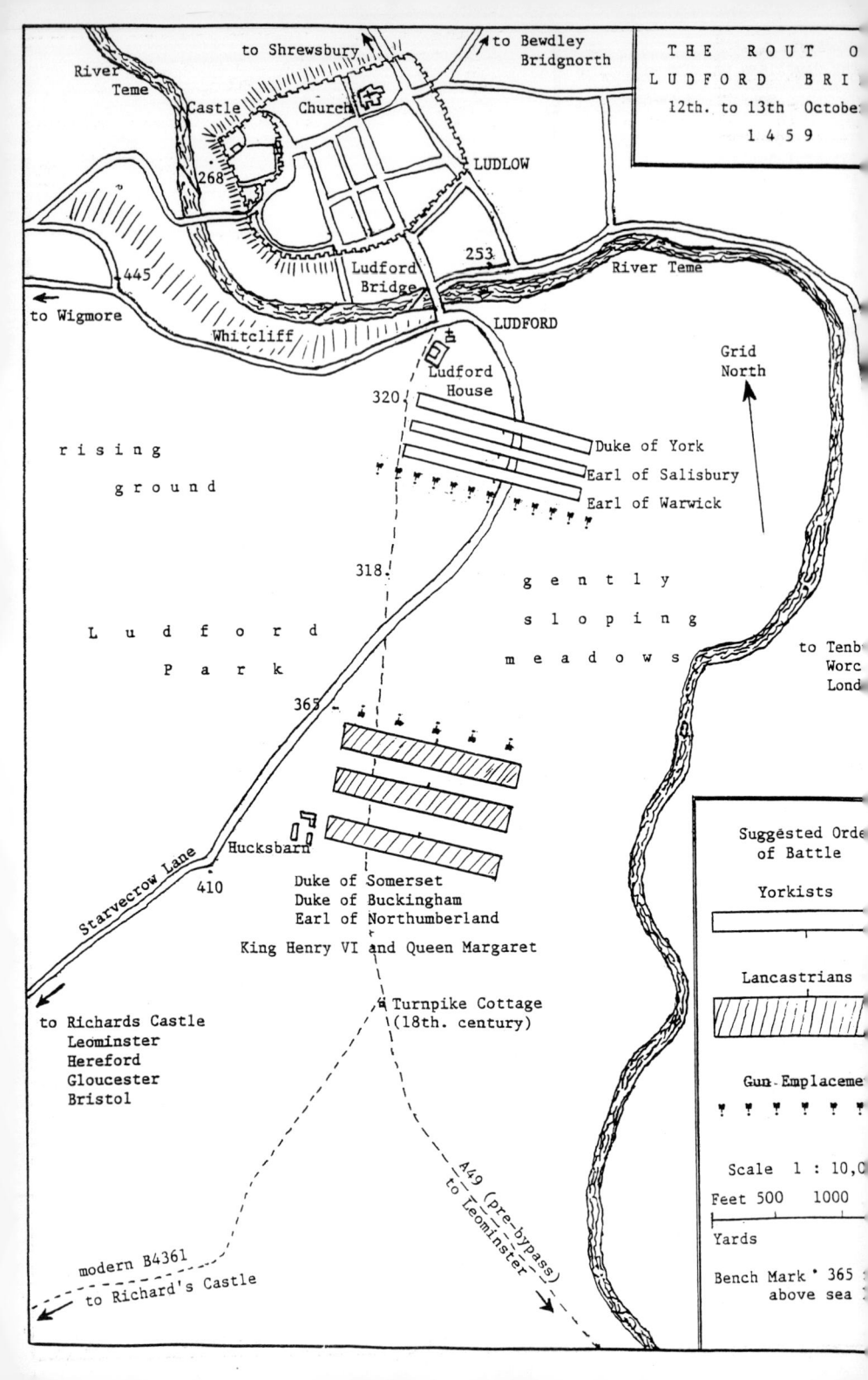

THE ROUT O[F]
LUDFORD BRI[DGE]
12th. to 13th Octobe[r]
1459

to Shrewsbury
to Bewdley
Bridgnorth

River Teme
Castle
Church
268
LUDLOW
253
River Teme

445
to Wigmore
Whitcliff
Ludford Bridge
LUDFORD
Ludford House
320

Grid North

Duke of York
Earl of Salisbury
Earl of Warwick

rising ground

318

Ludford Park

gently sloping meadows

to Tenb[ury]
Worc[ester]
Lond[on]

363
Hucksbarn
410
Starvecrow Lane

Duke of Somerset
Duke of Buckingham
Earl of Northumberland
King Henry VI and Queen Margaret

Turnpike Cottage
(18th. century)

to Richards Castle
Leominster
Hereford
Gloucester
Bristol

modern B4361
to Richard's Castle

A49 (pre-bypass)
to Leominster

Suggested Orde[r]
of Battle

Yorkists

Lancastrians

Gun Emplaceme[nt]

Scale 1 : 10,0[00]
Feet 500   1000
Yards

Bench Mark • 365 [feet]
above sea [level]

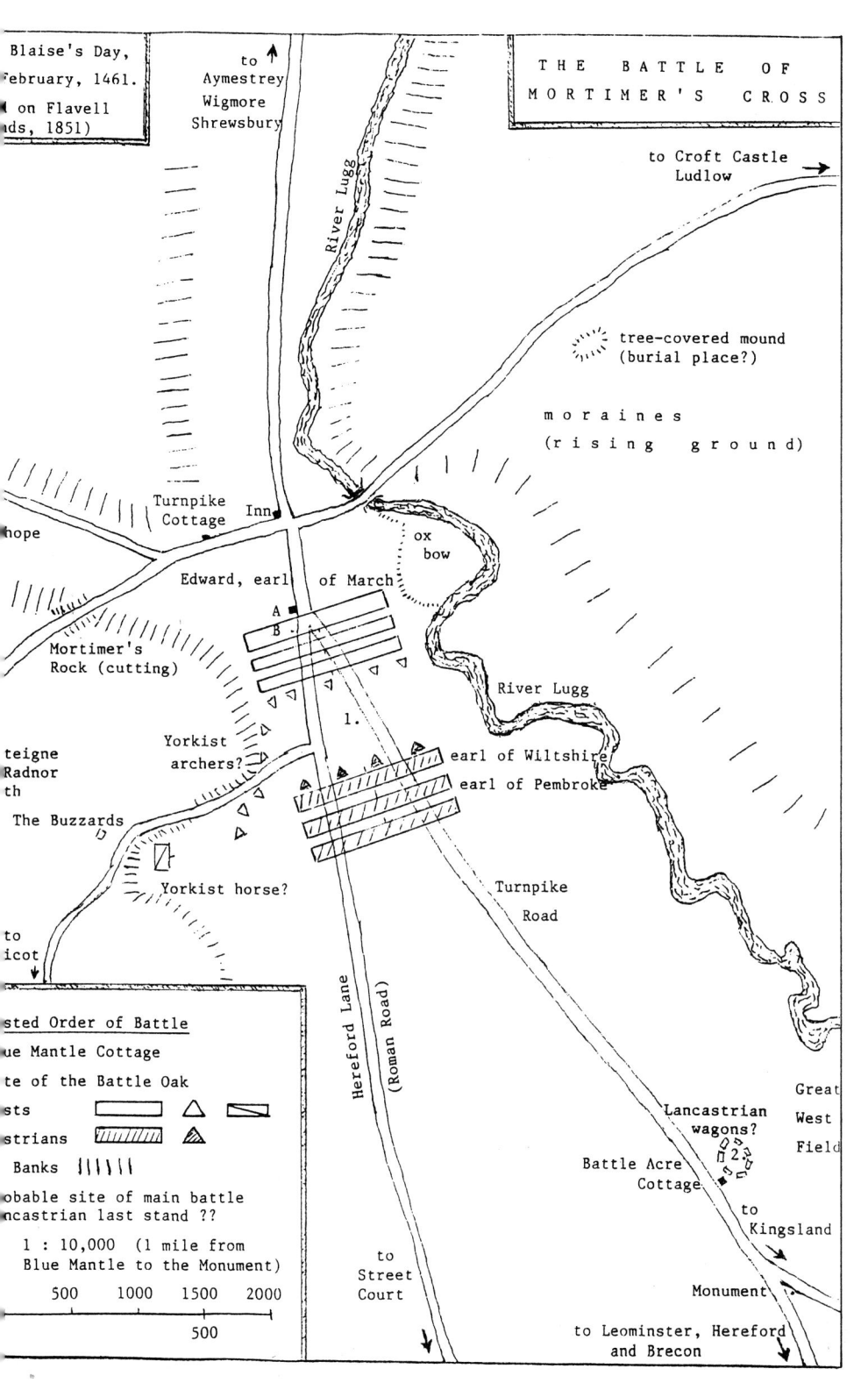

THE BATTLE OF MORTIMER'S CROSS

Blaise's Day,
February, 1461.
on Flavell
ds, 1851)

to Aymestrey
Wigmore
Shrewsbury

to Croft Castle
Ludlow

River Lugg

tree-covered mound
(burial place?)

moraines
(rising ground)

Turnpike Cottage
Inn
hope
ox bow

Edward, earl of March

A
B

Mortimer's Rock (cutting)

River Lugg

Yorkist archers?

1.

teigne
Radnor
th

earl of Wiltshire
earl of Pembroke

The Buzzards

Yorkist horse?

Turnpike Road

to icot

Hereford Lane (Roman Road)

sted Order of Battle
ue Mantle Cottage
te of the Battle Oak
sts
strians
Banks
obable site of main battle
ncastrian last stand ??

1 : 10,000 (1 mile from
Blue Mantle to the Monument)

500   1000   1500   2000
        500

Lancastrian wagons?
Battle Acre Cottage

Great West Field

to Kingsland

Monument

to Street Court

to Leominster, Hereford
and Brecon

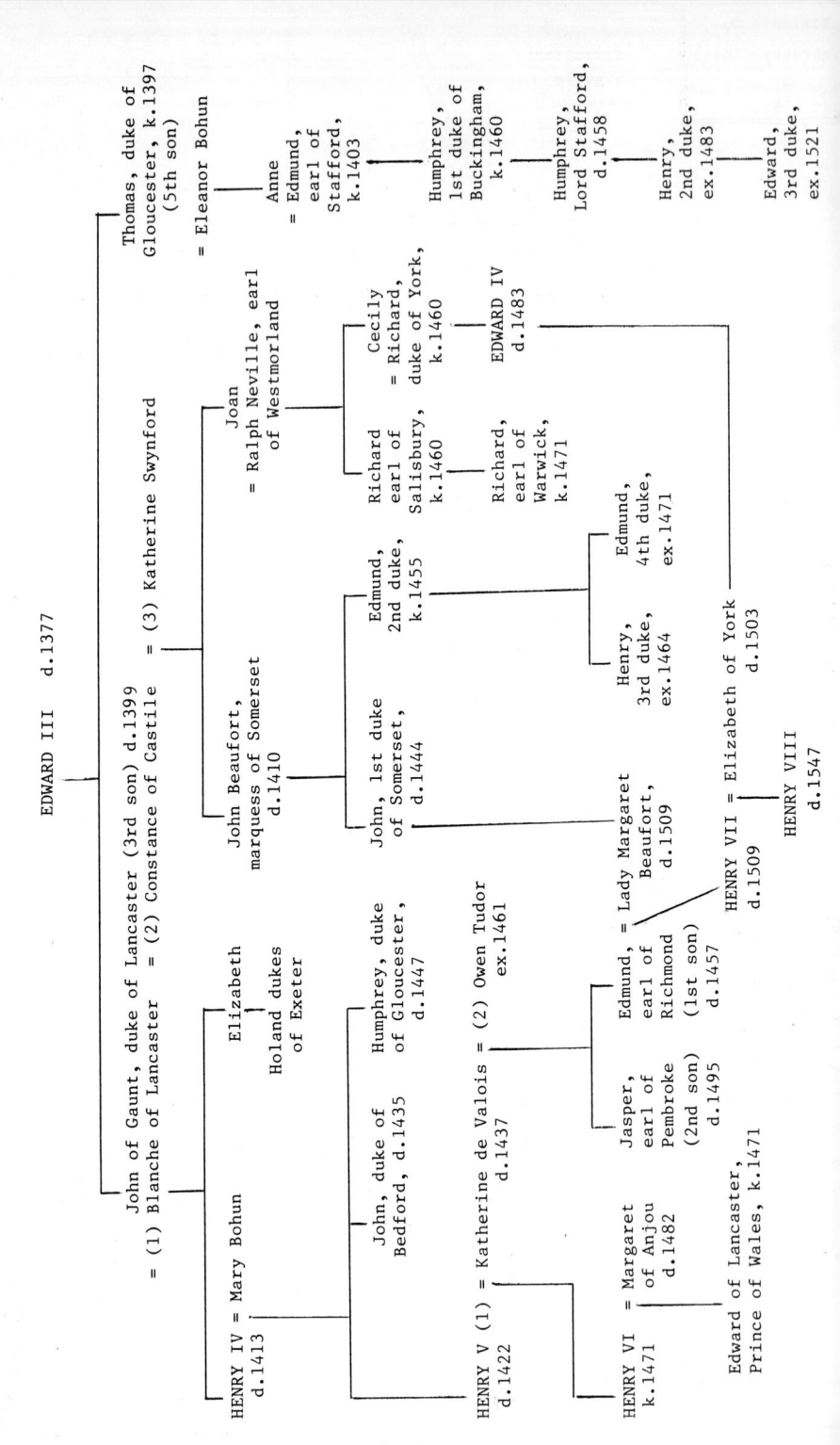

GENEALOGICAL TABLE 1   LANCASTER, BEAUFORT, TUDOR AND STAFFORD

EDWARD III d.1377

John of Gaunt, duke of Lancaster (3rd son) d.1399
= (1) Blanche of Lancaster = (2) Constance of Castile = (3) Katherine Swynford

Thomas, duke of Gloucester, k.1397 (5th son) = Eleanor Bohun

HENRY IV = Mary Bohun
d.1413

Elizabeth
Holand dukes of Exeter

John Beaufort, marquess of Somerset d.1410

Joan = Ralph Neville, earl of Westmorland

Anne = Edmund, earl of Stafford, k.1403

John, duke of Bedford, d.1435

Humphrey, duke of Gloucester, d.1447

John, 1st duke of Somerset, d.1444

Edmund, 2nd duke, k.1455

Richard, earl of Salisbury, k.1460

Cecily = Richard, duke of York, k.1460

Humphrey, 1st duke of Buckingham, k.1460

HENRY V (1) = Katherine de Valois = (2) Owen Tudor
d.1422   d.1437   ex.1461

Henry, 3rd duke, ex.1464

Edmund, 4th duke, ex.1471

Richard, earl of Warwick, k.1471

EDWARD IV d.1483

Humphrey, Lord Stafford, d.1458

HENRY VI = Margaret of Anjou
k.1471   d.1482

Jasper, earl of Pembroke (2nd son) d.1495

Edmund, earl of Richmond (1st son) d.1457 = Lady Margaret Beaufort, d.1509

Henry, 2nd duke, ex.1483

Edward of Lancaster, Prince of Wales, k.1471

HENRY VII = Elizabeth of York
d.1509   d.1503

Edward, 3rd duke, ex.1521

HENRY VIII
d.1547

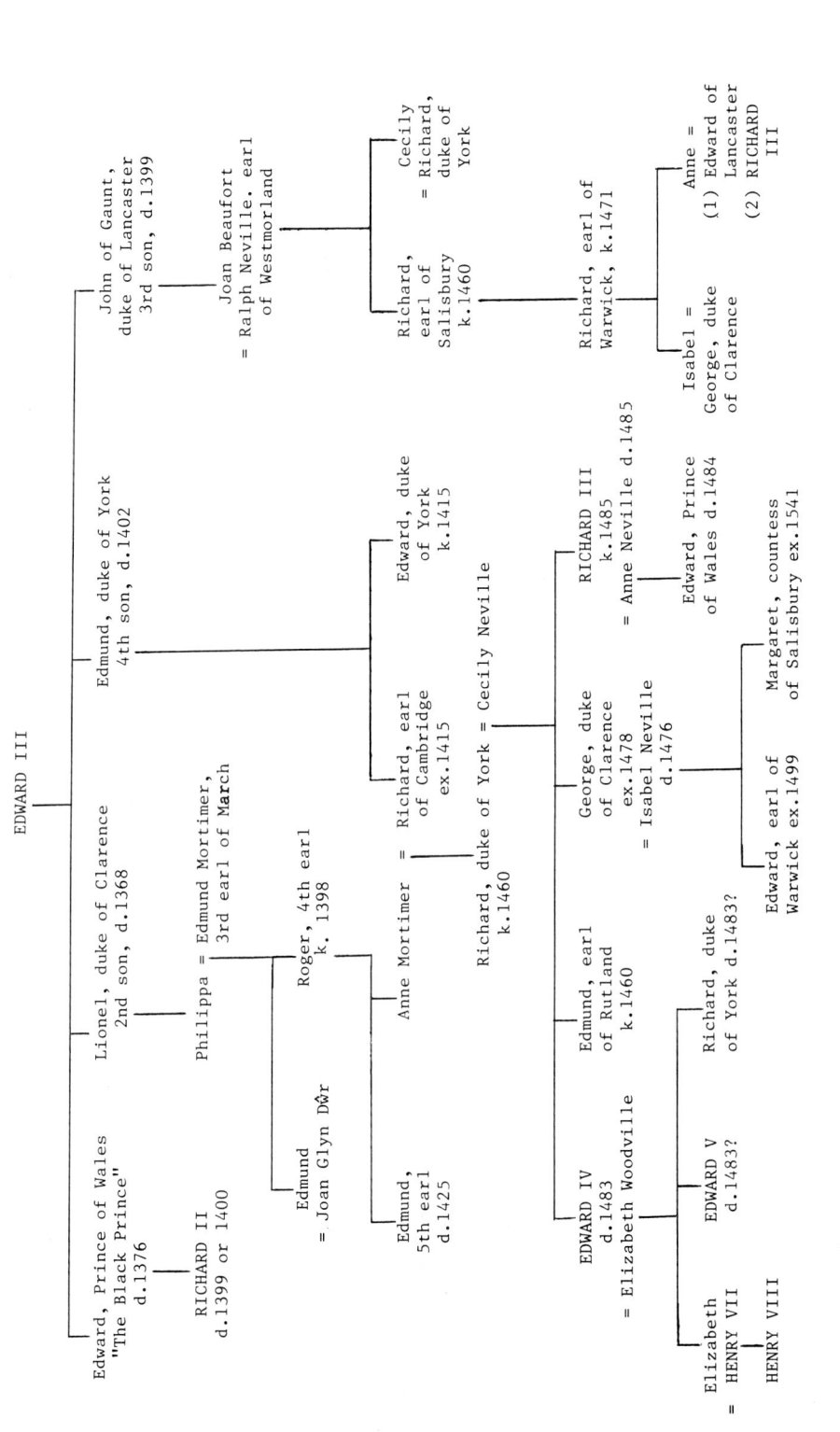

GENEALOGICAL TABLE 2   YORK, MORTIMER AND NEVILLE

EDWARD III
├── Edward, Prince of Wales "The Black Prince" d.1376
│   └── RICHARD II d.1399 or 1400
├── Lionel, duke of Clarence 2nd son, d.1368
│   └── Phillippa = Edmund Mortimer, 3rd earl of March
│   ├── Roger, 4th earl k.1398
│   │   ├── Edmund, 5th earl d.1425
│   │   └── Anne Mortimer = Richard, earl of Cambridge ex.1415
│   │   └── Richard, duke of York = Cecily Neville k.1460
│   │   ├── Edmund, earl of Rutland k.1460
│   │   ├── EDWARD IV d.1483 = Elizabeth Woodville
│   │   │   ├── Elizabeth = HENRY VII
│   │   │   │   └── HENRY VIII
│   │   │   ├── EDWARD V d.1483?
│   │   │   └── Richard, duke of York d.1483?
│   │   ├── George, duke of Clarence ex.1478 = Isabel Neville d.1476
│   │   │   ├── Edward, earl of Warwick ex.1499
│   │   │   └── Margaret, countess of Salisbury ex.1541
│   │   └── RICHARD III k.1485 = Anne Neville d.1485
│   │   └── Edward, Prince of Wales d.1484
│   └── Edmund = Joan Glyn Dŵr
├── Edmund, duke of York 4th son, d.1402
│   └── Edward, duke of York k.1415
└── John of Gaunt, duke of Lancaster 3rd son, d.1399
    └── Joan Beaufort = Ralph Neville, earl of Westmorland
        └── Cecily = Richard, duke of York
            └── Richard, earl of Salisbury k.1460
                └── Richard, earl of Warwick, k.1471
                    ├── Isabel = George, duke of Clarence
                    └── Anne = (1) Edward of Lancaster (2) RICHARD III

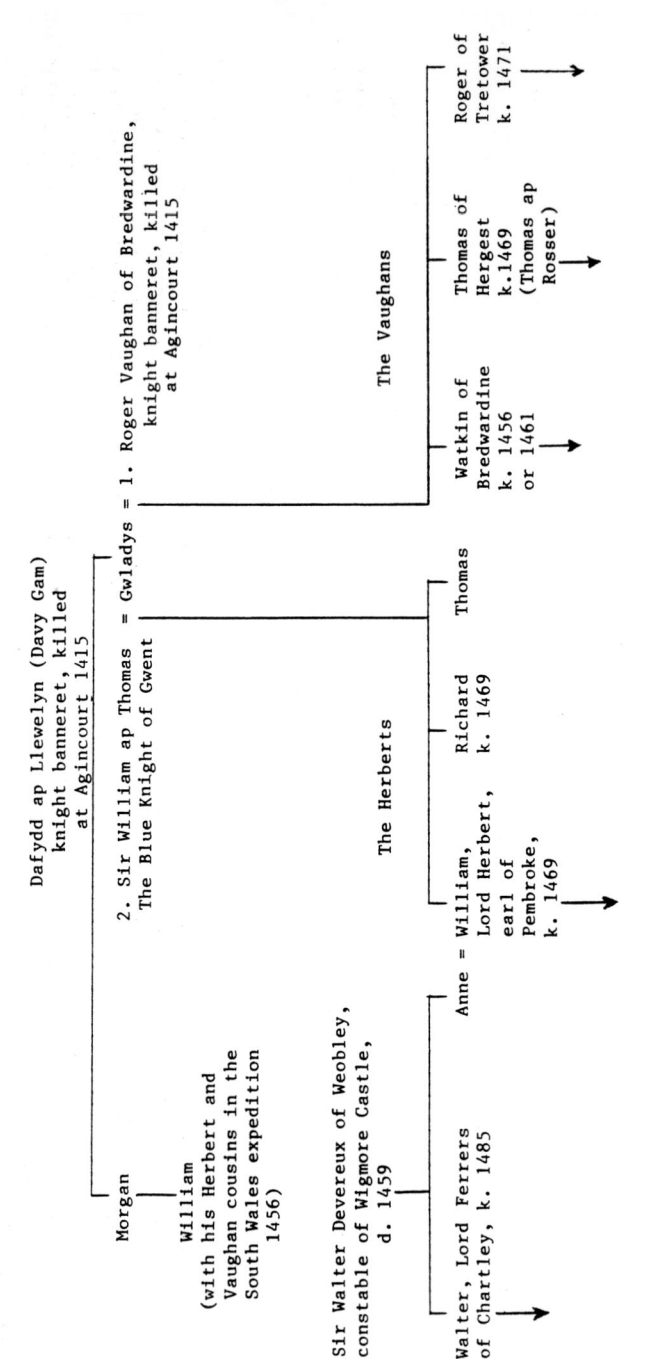

GENEALOGICAL TABLE 3   THE DESCENDANTS OF DAVY GAM

```
                    Dafydd ap Llewelyn (Davy Gam)
                          knight banneret, killed
                              at Agincourt 1415
                                      |
         ┌────────────────────────────┴────────────────────────────┐
         |                                                          |
  2. Sir William ap Thomas = Gwladys = 1. Roger Vaughan of Bredwardine,
     The Blue Knight of Gwent                knight banneret, killed
                                                 at Agincourt 1415
         |                                                |
  ┌──────┴──────┐                                         |
  |             |                                         |
Morgan                                                The Vaughans
                                                          |
William                                   ┌───────────────┼───────────────┐
(with his Herbert and                     |               |               |
Vaughan cousins in the                 Watkin of      Thomas of       Roger of
South Wales expedition                 Bredwardine    Hergest         Tretower
1456)                                  k. 1456        k.1469          k. 1471
                                       or 1461        (Thomas ap
Sir Walter Devereux of Weobley,                        Rosser)
constable of Wigmore Castle,              →               →               →
d. 1459
         |
         |            The Herberts
         |
  ┌──────┼──────────────────┬──────────────┐
  |                         |              |
 Anne = William,        Richard,        Thomas
        Lord Herbert,   k. 1469
        earl of
        Pembroke,
        k. 1469
  |                         →
Walter, Lord Ferrers
of Chartley, k. 1485
  →
```

Note   This table has mainly been taken from the one in The Poetical Works of Lewis Glyn Cothi, edited for the Cymmrodorion (Oxford, 1837): also for Robinson, Mansions, page 163 – the Vaughans of Hergest. A seventeenth century saying, "We are all cousins in Herefordshire", is borne out by any fully detailed pedigree of a Herefordshire family; the Vaughans, Herberts, Crofts, Devereux, Baskervilles, Cornewalls and so on were all interrelated. It is not clear whether Richard Herbert and Thomas of Hergest died on the battlefield or the block, like their brother; the years of Warwick's supremacy were grim ones for the House of Davy Gam, although William Herbert and the three Vaughans had very many descendants. Margaret Vaughan of Hergest, lady-in-waiting to Queen Elizabeth, married the great Sir John Hawkins, and founded the grammar school at Kington, now known as the Lady Hawkins School.

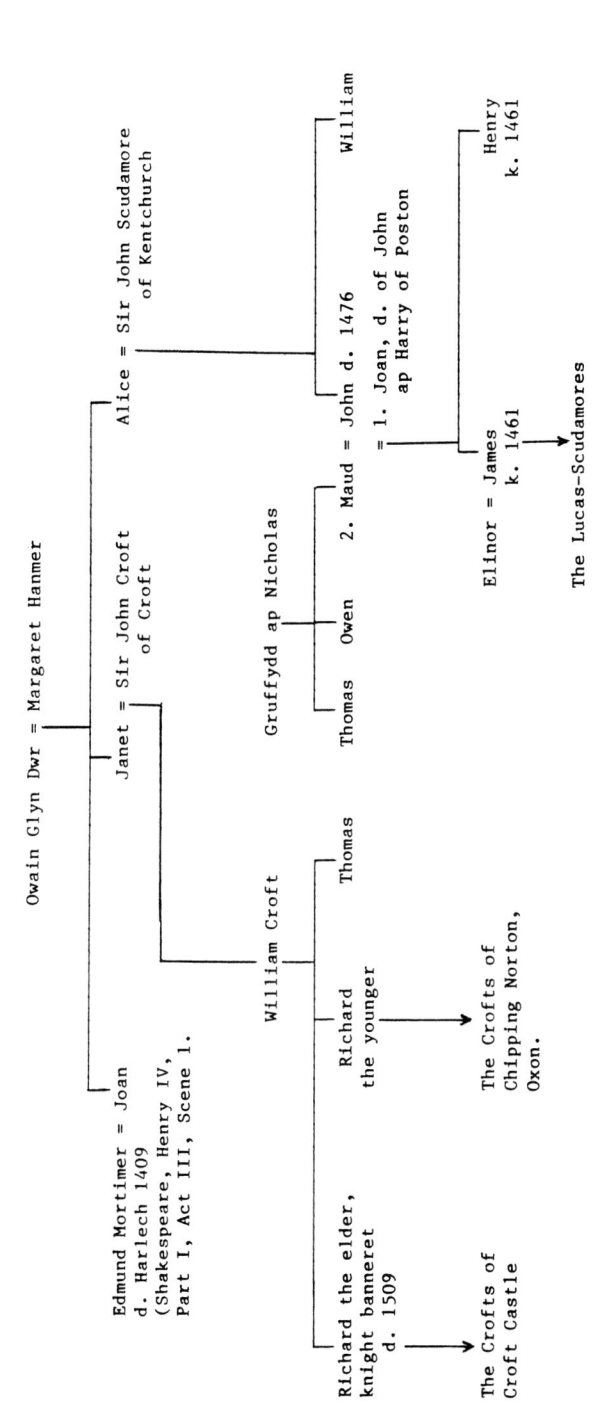

```
                          Owain Glyn Dwr = Margaret Hanmer
                                         |
        ┌────────────────────────┬───────┴──────────────┐
Edmund Mortimer = Joan    Janet = Sir John Croft    Alice = Sir John Scudamore
d. Harlech 1409                   of Croft                  of Kentchurch
(Shakespeare, Henry IV,
Part I, Act III, Scene 1.)
```

Gruffydd ap Nicholas

```
                    |                                    |
    ┌───────────┬───┴──────┐             ┌───────┬───────┼──────────────┬──────────┐
William Croft  Thomas   Richard        Thomas  Owen   2. Maud = John d. 1476   William
               the      the younger                    1. Joan, d. of John
                                                          ap Harry of Poston
```

```
Richard the elder,                                      Elinor = James      Henry
knight banneret                                                  k. 1461    k. 1461
d. 1509
                                                        The Lucas-Scudamores
The Crofts of        The Crofts of
Croft Castle         Chipping Norton,
                     Oxon.
```

Note   This table is based on Robinson, *Mansions*, page 81, the Crofts, and page 155, the Scudamores of Kentchurch: also on O.G.S. Croft, *The House of Croft of Croft Castle* (Hereford, 1949), pages 28 to 47. The matrimonial affairs of the second Sir John Scudamore look complicated, and are. Robinson shows his son as married to a daughter of Griffith Nicholas of Newton, probably Gruffydd ap Nicholas; but both H.T. Evans (page 95) and R.A. Griffiths (*Henry VI*, page 735) say that Sir John also married a daughter of Gruffydd, thereby sealing his alliance with Jasper Tudor. James Scudamore's grandfather John ap Harry or Parry was probably an uncle of Henry ap Gruffydd, who was an associate of William Herbert, and fought at Mortimer's Cross. Robinson does not make this clear, but Henry VIII disapproved of what he called "these aps and naps", and Welshmen began to adopt anglicisations like Parry and Williams. Blanche Parry, grand-daughter of Henry ap Gruffydd, was gentlewoman of the bedchamber to Elizabeth as princess and queen; she died in 1589, aged 82.

Some Important Dates

1399 Henry VI took the crown from Richard II
1402 Owain Glyn Dwr's victory at Pilleth
1403 Battle of Shrewsbury
1415 Battle of Agincourt
1422 Accession of Henry VI
1445 Marriage of Henry VI and Margaret of Anjou
1450 Loss of Normandy; Jack Cade's Rebellion
1453 Battle of Castillon; loss of Gascony; Henry VI's madness
1455 First battle of St. Albans
1456 Yorkist invasion of South Wales
1459 Rout of Ludford Bridge
1460 Battles of Northampton and Wakefield
1461 Battles of Mortimer's Cross, second St. Albans and Towton; Edward IV took crown from Henry VI
1469 Warwick's rebellion; battle of Edgecote
1470 Warwick restored Henry VI
1471 Edward IV's victories at Barnet and Tewkesbury; his restoration
1483 Death of Edward IV; Richard III took crown from Edward V
1485 Battle of Bosworth; death of Richard III; Henry VII took crown

Selected Bibliography (short titles)

Contemporary and Tudor

Calendar of Close Rolls, 1454-61 (1967)
Calendar of Patent Rolls, 1452-61 (1911); 1461-67 (1897)
Calendar of State Papers (Milan), Vol. 1 (1913)
Parliamentary Rolls, Vol. V – Henry VI (1832)
Proceedings and Ordinances of the Privy Council, Vol. VI (1837)
Brie F.W.D. ed. *The Brut Chronicle* (1908)
Daniel, Samuel *The Civil Wars between York and Lancaster* (1595)
Davies, J.S. ed. *An English Chronicle 1377-1461* (Camden Society 1856)
Ellis, H. ed. *Robert Fabyan's Chronicles* (1811)
Ellis, H. ed. *Edward Hall's Chronicles* (1809)
Gairdner, J. ed. *Gregory's Chronicle* (Camden Society 1876)
Gairdner, J. ed. *Three fifteenth Century Chronicles* (Camden Society 1880), including *A Short English Chronicle*
Gairdner, J. ed. *The Paston Letters* (1904)
Harris, G.L. and M.A. ed. *John Benet's Chronicle* (1972)
Harvey, J.H. ed. *William Worcester: Itineraries* (1969)
Shakespeare, William *Historical Plays* (1590-99)
Thomas, A.H. and I.D. Thornley ed. *The Great Chronicle of London* (1938)
Waurin, Jean de *Chronicles* (1891)

Eighteenth and Nineteenth Centuries

Battle Monument, Kingsland (1799)
Brooke, R. *Visits to fields of Battle in England* (1857)
Duncumb, J. *The History of the County of Hereford* (1804)
Edmunds, Flavell *The Battle of Mortimer's Cross* (1851)
Price, Jonathan *The Leominster Guide* (1808)
Robinson, C.J. *The Castles of Herefordshire* (1869)
Robinson, C.J. *The Manors and Mansions of Herefordshire* (1873)
Symonds, W.S. *Malvern Chase* (1881)
Wright, T. *The History and Antiquities of Ludlow* (1826)

The Twentieth Century

Armstrong, C.A.J. *England, France and Burgundy in the fifteenth Century* (1983)
La Borderie and Pocquet, *Histoire de Bretagne Vol IV* (Rennes, 1906)
Clive, Mary *This Sun of York* (1973)
Cook, Donald R. *Lancastrians and Yorkists: The Wars of the Roses* (1984)
Evans, H.T. *Wales and the Wars of the Roses* (1915)
Fairburn, Neil *The Battlefields of Britain* (1983)
Gillingham, John *The Wars of the Roses* (1981)
Goodman, Anthony *The Wars of the Roses* (1981)
Green, Howard *The Battlefields of Britain and Ireland* (1973)
Green, Howard *The Central Midlands* (The Regional Military Histories, 1974)
Griffiths, R.A. *The Reign of Henry VI* (1981)
Griffiths, R.A. and Roger Thomas, *The Making of the Tudor Dynasty* (1985)
Jacob, E.F. *Oxford History of England: The fifteenth Century* (1961)
Kendal, P.M. *Warwick the Kingmaker* (1957)
Kinross, John *Discovering Battlefields of England* (1968)
de Laigue, Rene, *La Noblesse Bretonne aux XVe et XVIe Siècles* (Rennes, 1902)
Lander, J.R. *England 1450-1509* (1980)
Lloyd, David, and Peter Klein, *Ludlow* (1984)
McFarlane, K.B. *England in the Fifteenth Century* (1981)
Ross, Charles *Edward IV* (1974)
Ross, Charles *The Wars of the Roses* (1976)
Senior, Michael ed., Thomas Malory's *Le Morte d'Arthur*, abridged with modern spelling (1980)
Smurthwaite, David *Battlefields of Britain* (1984)
Storey, R.L. *The End of the House of Lancaster* (1966; 2nd. ed. 1986)
Thomas, Roger, unpublished Ph.D. Thesis on Jasper Tudor, University College, Swansea (1971)
Weaver, Richard and Ann Radnor *The Battle of Mortimer's Cross* (by Spot Video: Hereford, 1987)
Wedgwood, J.C. *History of Parliament: Biographies of the members of the Commons House, 1439-1509* (1938)